4/86

729   JONES, FREDERIC H.   (FREDERIC
            HICKS)
        INTERIOR DESIGN GRAPHICS.
c1983

82   8 88 89 90   94

  92   93   99   00

98   09

    01

DEMCO

INTERIOR DESIGN GRAPHICS

BASICS
EXAMPLES
STANDARDS

INTERIOR DESIGN GRAPHICS

BASICS
EXAMPLES
STANDARDS

FREDERIC H. JONES

Published by William Kaufmann, Inc.
95 First Street
Los Altos, California 94022

10   9   8   7   6   5   4   4   3   2   1

Printed in the United States of America

Library of Congress Cataloging in Publication Data
Jones, Frederic H. (Frederic Hicks) 1944–
      Interior design graphics.

      Bibliography: p.
      1. Interior decoration—Study and
teaching.   I. Title.
NK2116.4.J66   1983   729   83-22207
ISBN 0-86576-061-6

CONTENTS

INTRODUCTION

This book has been developed and tested over several years and with hundreds of students of interior design graphics. It is meant to fill the gap left by a shelf full of other sources.

There are many books on drafting and architectural graphics, and recently several interior design drafting books have appeared. None of them, however, present a simple explanation of design for the absolute beginner. Another important omission in these books is a collection of examples of professional drafting with which students and other professionals can compare their work and ideas. This comparison of notes is one of the best teaching methods. Finally, most texts do not present standards. While it is impossible to be comprehensive in a book of this size, I have provided a significant compilation of standards as well as references to enable you to research and add to your own standards collection.

I hope this book will be not only a basic drafting text but that it will continue to be useful to students and professional designers as a reference text of standards an examples, and a source of ideas and information.

TOOLS

Tools are more than tools! They are a romantic symbol of what we do and how we do it. Tools are a badge of our profession I cannot stress too much the importance of appropriate and quality tools. On the other hand, tools need not be the most expensive available. Moderately priced and well-made tools are available and can be as effective and satisfying as the gold plated, engraved, presentation variety.

I have outlined here the basic tools you will encounter as an interior design draftsman, as well as many optional ones. Become familiar with the field and keep your eye out in the art supply store for new products. You will find, if you are like me, that you will acquire a collection of tools that will be occasionally useful, and a few treasured favorites which will be your mainstays. My favorite red drafting pencil and a tinted 3" adjustable triangle go with me like Linus's blanket.

A sturdy drafting board, either a lap or table type is necessary for serious drafting. A metal edge is required if a t-square is to be used. The surface should be covered with a drafting cover such as "Borco" plastic for maximum utility. The surface should never be cut on or punctured with tacks. Only drafting tape is acceptable for fastening drawings. The board should be larger than the largest sheet of paper you expect to use. A typical board size for interior design drawing is 30" x 42".

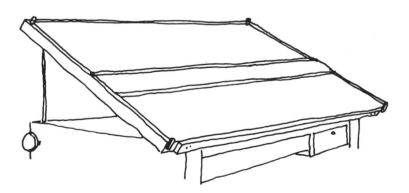

The parallel edge such as "Mayline" or "Para-draft" is mounted with cable on the drawing board. It moves smoothly up and down remaining parallel but without the hand tension required of the t-square. This is much preferred over the t-square for serious drafters. The kind you mount yourself on top of the board is much smoother than the one that comes integrated with the board by the factory. It is simple to install yourself.

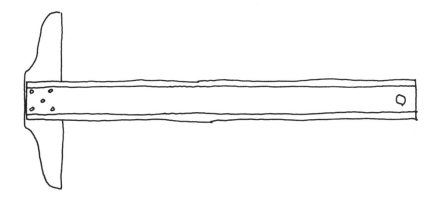

The t-square is used to draw lines parallel to the drawing board front edge. It is snuggled tightly against the drawing board edge and the pencil is drawn across the plastic edge to make a straight and parallel line. Angled and perpendicular lines are constructed with a triangle. A wooden t-square with a clear plastic edge is the preferred one for drafting.

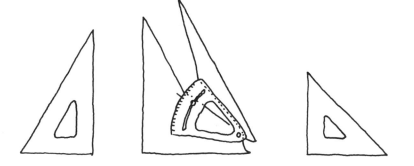

Triangles are used for drawing lines other than horizontal. They are standard in 45°, 30°/60°, and adjustable in many sizes. The adjustable is the basic tool and an 8" triangle would be a good first choice. A large 12" 45° triangle would be a good choice for long lines. A 3" 30/60° is good for hatching and lettering.

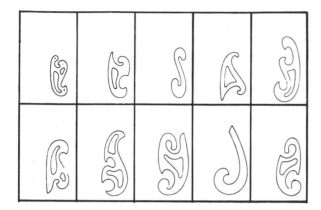

French curves are used to draw curved segments of objects or plans. They are drawn against with pencil or pen after an appropriate segment is selected. A selection of two or three is usually enough for interior design drafting.

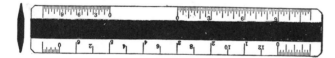

Scale rules come in triangular and flat styles and in 6" and 12" lengths. 1/4" scale means that a foot in the actual building would be represented by 1/4" on the plan. The scale rule makes thinking in scale much easier for in the 1/4" scale, the rule is marked just as if each 1/4" is a foot and these "small" feet are broken into 12 "inches" Other scales like 1/8", 1/4", 1/2", 3/8", 1-1/2", and 3" are represented. A 12" triangular scale rule is the basic scale rule.

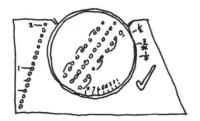

A lettering guide is used to make light pencil guidelines to assure neat and uniform lettering on plans and drawings. This is used with hand lettering, not templates. Instructions for its use come with the device.

The lead holder with loose lead is superior to wood clad pencils for drafting. It can hold any hardness of lead and can quickly be changed and sharpened with the lead pointer. "F" lead is standard for all-around drafting.

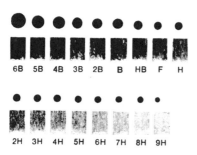

6B 5B 4B 3B 2B B HB F H

2H 3H 4H 5H 6H 7H 8H 9H

Graphite (black) drawing pencil: The term "lead" pencil is a misnomer. The principal ingredient of most drawing pencils is graphite, a black mineral variety of carbon. The degree of hardness is indicated by a standard code; this chart approximates diameters of 17 degrees.

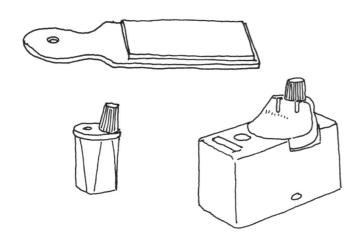

The pencil pointer is as basic as the pencil holder and lead to the drafter. The basic type with steel cutter is recommended over other types. It has several bushings for different pencil diameters and has a gauge for blunt or sharp cutting. A sand paper board is good for rendering and sketching. It can chisel and blunt leads for special techniques.

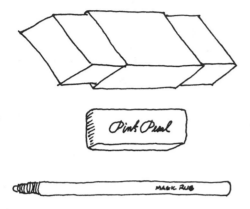

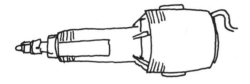

The Magic Rub and Pink Pearl are the basic erasers for drafting used in pencil, block or plug for electric erasers.

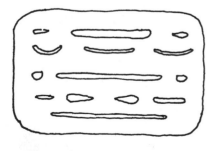

The electric eraser is a basic tool of the drafter and comes both in cord and cordless types. It saves time and makes a much neater tracing than conventional erasers.

A stainless steel eraser shield is used to mask off parts of the drawing you don't want to erase and to expose those you do. It's also used for making dashed lines. Just lay it over the pencil mark with the error exposed through an opening and erase. The steel part protects the good line and makes a much neater correction.

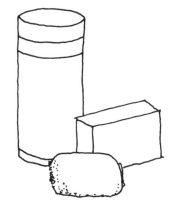

Dry cleaning pad is sprinkled on the tracing as the drafter works. It keeps the tracing clean of graphite smudges. It is best not to rub it on the paper. The material is similar to eraser dust and absorbs the loose graphite dust that can smudge your paper.

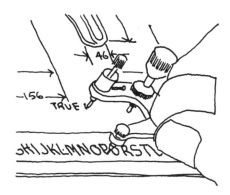

Leroy Lettering Sets use a plastic template to guide a scriber with an ink pen to letter many sizes and styles of type on plans and drawings. This is an excellent way for neat titles. Sets come with as few as three lettering templates and a scribe.

Drafting tape is not as sticky as masking tape and is used to hold tracing paper to the drafting board without damaging the paper or the drawing surface. Drafting tape is also less likely to leave gum on the paper and drafting board. 3/4 inch wide tape is the best all around size.

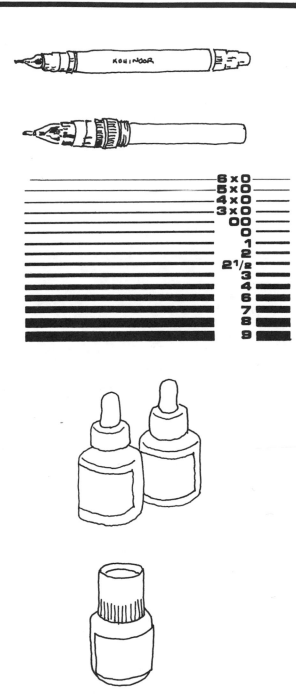

The technical pen is the basic ink drawing instrument.   It is easy to use and comes in many line widths for various needs. It produces a uniform line width.   A good basic set would include a 00 (very fine), 0, 2½, then add 000, 1, 2, and 4.   00 is a good sketching instrument to use when you occasionally need to draft lines in ink for presentations and the like.

Colored drawing ink, one of the most versatile mediums, is used for many purposes. It comes in two basic types: translucent and opaque.   Black india ink (waterproof) is opaque and best for working drawings, fine line work and washes.   It is free from dye and contains carbon as a pigment. Special inks (like "acetate" ink) are made for use on water repellent drafting surfaces without "crawling", such as acetate, Mylar film, Lumarith, tracing cloth and similar **plastic materials.**

Drawing inks have a reasonable degree of permanence if kept from sunlight or strong diffused light.   Shellack is the usual waterproofing ingredient--therefore it is necessary to thoroughly clean pens, instruments and brushes after use.   Several pen cleaners listed are good for this purpose.

To dilute black ink, add pure water with four drops of aqual ammonia to the ounce. Tap water will suffice for washes which are applied at once.   To dilute colored inks, use pure water only.   Never add any acid or mix ink brands.

A drafting brush is ideal for dusting erasure leavings and graphite dust off your tracings and drawing board.

A flexible curve can take the place of French curves and at the same time allow you to customize your own shapes and transfer a shape from one drawing to another.

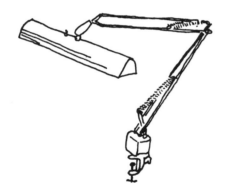

A good drafting board lamp is mandatory. One that gives good strong light with an opaque shade that prevents direct glare is best. Also a flexible one that can move about to prevent reflected glare is important.

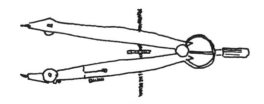

A Bow compass is handy for drawing circles and arcs. This can substitute for a circle template and will work with both pencil and ink.

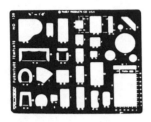

"ABC"

Scale   1/8" =   Size   4-7/8"   x   3-1/16"
Door swings, circles, etc.

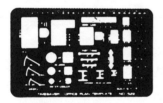

FURNITURE

Scale: 1/4"-1'.   For quickly visualizing
furniture space and adaptability, 65 pieces
of furniture with width, depth and height
of   each.   Size: 5-1/4"   x   6-3/4".

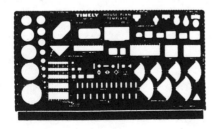

OFFICE PLAN

Office equipment at 1/4" scale.
Size: 4-1/2" x 7".

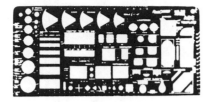

"ABC"

Scale 1/8" = Size 4-7/8" x 3-1/16"
Door swings, circles, etc.

PAPER

BASIC PAPER TERMS

TOOTH is the arrangement of fibers in the surfaces of paper which form little peaks or depressions referred to as "teeth". Created by an unevenness of surface in the manufacture, these peaks actually appear from the depression of the pencil, lead, crayon or pastel. More toothing makes for a rougher surface...bulkier and more absorbent. There is also more light reflection as the tooth increases. The term "bite" is also often used to describe this textured result.

FEEL is used to express the reaction to physically handling a paper; its comparative bulk, resiliency, finish, "snap", weight, etc.

GRAIN is the direction the fibers of a paper run as it is manufactured. It affects surface, directional patterns, folding, tear qualities and dimensionable stability.

HARD is used to describe high finish but really indicates a high degree of water resistance imparted by surface sizing.

SLICK is used to express a smooth vellum-like finish, usually stated as "high" or "plate" finish.

LB. SUBSTANCE refers to the weight of a paper in pounds. The lb. designation of a paper is determined by the weight of a ream (500 sheets) in its basic size. For example: the basic size of bond papers is 17" x 22". 500 sheets of a light-weight bond in this size would weigh 16 pounds...hence, 16-lb. paper. 500 sheets of a ledger bond (heavier weight) in this size would weigh 32 pounds...hence, 32-lb. paper. The basic sizes of papers vary from grade to grade, arbitrarily dictated by paper mills many years ago to accommodate the sizes of printing presses.

Artists' papers can range from 16-lb. and lighter (tracing paper, for example) up to 300-lb. (heavy watercolor paper).

RAG CONTENT indicates that a paper contains a percentage of rag or cotton pulp, from 25% to 100%. The richness and permanence of a sheet varies with the percentage of the rag content, and makes for better erasability.

BRISTOL BOARD SURFACES

HIGH SURFACE (Smooth or Plate Finish).   A uniformly overall, smooth finish; takes the most delicate line techniques in pen or pencil.

MEDIUM SURFACE (Kid or Vellum Finish).   A "toothy", slightly textured finish for almost any technique: line and wash, air brush, tempera, acrylic, pastel, etc.

Either surface withstands repeated erasures and reworking without feathering.

ILLUSTRATION, MAT, MOUNT BOARD AND PAPER THICKNESSES

ST Single Thick (Appx. 1/16" or 60 pts.)
DT Double Thick (Appx. 1/8" or 110 pts.)
TT Triple Thick (Appx. 3/16" or 165 pts.)

POINT .001 (a thousandth of an inch) The thickness of some boards and papers are indicated by points.

BOND PAPER 16-lb. is approximately .003 points thick

LEDGER PAPER 32-lb. is approximately .006 points thick.

PAPER QUANTITIES

QUIRE: 25 sheets
REAM: 500 sheets

DRAFTING PAPER : Two kinds are used in interior design drafting extensively. The first is roll tracing paper that comes in white and yellow, and in various widths-18" is recommended.   This is inexpensive and is used for under- and over-lays, layouts and sketching.   The second type is 16 or 20 lb., 100% rag drafting vellum for finished work.   This comes in plain and pre-boardered in many sizes--18" x 24" and 24" x 30" are the most common.   The most popular brands are Clearprint #1000, Albanene and Teledine Natural.   The pre-boardered kind with end titleblocks are the most common for architecture and interior design.   The type with the blue grids is most commonly used for engineering.   It is usually divided into 10ths or 8ths.

PAPER FINISHES

These listings are intended for quick reference purposes, and include the most common words used in the art materials field. Consider these terms as a general guide. There are other words (of more specialized usage) that are used to describe finishes.

SMOOTH Usually described by the following terms:

Clay	Plate
Glazed	Smooth
High	Super
Hot Press	Super Calendered

MEDIUM Usually described by the following terms:

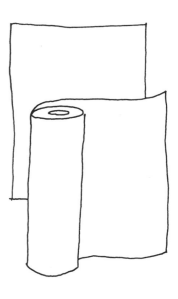

Cold Press	Regular
Dull	Satin
Eggshell	Slightly Grained
Kid	Unglazed
Matte	Vellum
Medium	Velour
Parchment	

ROUGH Usually described by the following terms:

Antique	Irregular
Coarse	Laid
Cockle	Machine
Embossed	Rough
Felt	

MUSEUM (RAG) BOARD

A specially formulated board used primarily by conservators, professional picture framers and others who are concerned about the longevity of works of art. It is acid-free (pH) neutral; usually made in white or off-white. Neither acidic nor alkaline, museum board does not contain chemicals which will stain the art by contact. It is suggested that this board be used for the mounting and framing of original lithographs and historic or valuable documents.

BLUEPRINTING

"Blueprinting" is a process of inexpensively reproducing an original drawing. This process allows the designer, who draws plans, details and other types of drawings on transparent or translucent paper, to have one or one-hundred copies to give to the client and contractors, and still protect the valuable original.

In times past, architects paid people to make "tracings" of their original drawings to give to the contractors. This process was supplanted by the "blueprinting" process and left us with the term "tracing" which is still used to describe that original drawing on translucent paper. The "blueprinting" process itself has since been largely replaced by a much more inexpensive process called "Diazo".

Diazo is a positive-to-positive process, rather than a positive-to-negative one like "blueprinting". It is a relatively dry process. Special machines are used to expose the "tracing" and a sensitive paper to ultra violet light. Then the sensitive copy is developed into a final copy. These "Diazo" copies come in blue line, brown and black line prints on bond paper, heavy "presentation" paper, or vellum (called Sepias). Mylar prints are also available. The prints are usually made on a white background. The clarity of the background depends on a high contrast between the lines drawn on the tracing and the vellum on which it is drawn. This is the reason you should make clear and dark lines in your original. Very light lettering guidelines and light blue colored pencil lines are virtually invisible to the "Diazo" machine and can be ignored when you prepare your tracing for reproduction.

It is important that you understand this reproduction process for it is the standard one for which you will prepare your originals. It is useful to visit a local graphics reproduction company and ask them to show you all their "tricks".

Another process that will become useful as you become more adept is Xerox 2080 enlargement or reduction of your drawings. Details may also be Xeroxed or printed on stick-back plastic and placed on your drawing. This replaces repeated tracings of a standard detail from sheet to sheet.

It is also important to note that the "Sepia" copies as well as the Xerox 2080 copies on vellum can serve as the base of additional tracings and Diazo reproductions for these "second originals" are indistinguishable from the "first originals". They may also be erased! I always make a Base plan, then make several "Sepia" second originals that become the ground on which to layout the Reflected Ceiling, Furniture, Electrical, and other sheets. This means that much of the work is done by the blueprint company and I don't have to trace the walls over and over again. The cost is very reasonable when compared to your hourly fee!

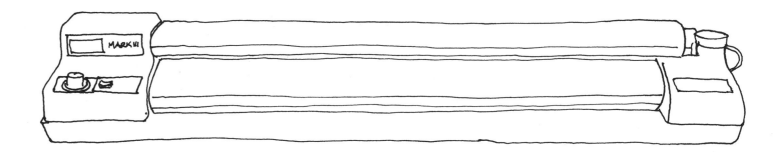

SYMBOLS

人 represents man in Chinese characters. "3" can stand for ♋♋♋. And 🚗
is obviously an automobile, though very simplified. All these are examples of
symbols which we come to recognize as second nature. The symbols of architectural drawing are similar. They are simplifications of the way something would
actually look but with only the essential details, like the automobile drawing above.
Here are some examples of <u>plan symbols</u>:

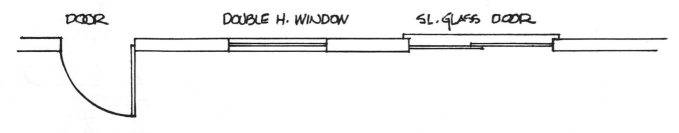

SCALE

Even with the simplification of these symbols it would be both difficult and expensive to draw a plan at full size, besides requiring quite a drawing board and t-square! So designers and architects have elected to "scale" down the drawing by substituting a smaller measurement for a larger one. For example, 1/8" instead of 1 foot, or 1 centimeter instead of 1 meter. This is written: 1/4" = 1'-0". 1/4", 1/8", and 1/2" are common scales in interior design but others are sometimes used as well. To aid in converting to scales easily and with accuracy, a <u>scale</u> ruler is used.

To use the scale rule, place the ruler using whatever scale is indicated (usually 1/4"). Center the zero on the scale on one of the points you are measuring and read the footage at the other point. If it reads between two foot dimensions (i.e., 24 or 25), move the <u>smaller</u> dimension to the second point and now the zero will be off the first mark. Notice to the outside of the zero there are smaller marks. These indicate inches and fractions of inches. If you add the inches between the zero and the mark, of the foot dimension over the second mark, you will have the scale dimension (i.e., 24' 6-1/2").

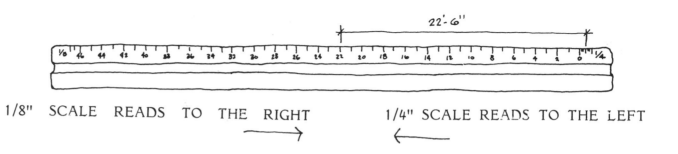

1/8" SCALE READS TO THE RIGHT   1/4" SCALE READS TO THE LEFT

FURNITURE TEMPLATES

ROUND COCTAIL TABLE

DIAMETER	HEIGHT
24"	16"
30"	15"
36"	16"
42"	15"
48"	16"

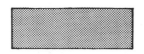

COCKTAIL TABLE

WIDTH	DEPTH	HEIGHT
35"	19"	17"
50"	18"	15"
54"	20"	15"
56"	21"	16"
57"	19"	15"
58"	20"	15"
61"	21"	17"

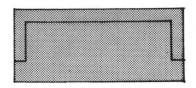

SOFA

WIDTH	DEPTH	HEIGHT
72"	36"	28"
76"	35"	35"
84"	36"	37"
87"	31"	31"
88"	32"	29"
91"	32"	30"

CORNER TABLE

WIDTH	DEPTH	HEIGHT
28"	28"	20"
30"	30"	15"

END TABLE

WIDTH	DEPTH	HEIGHT
21"	28"	20"
22"	28"	21"
26"	20"	21"
27"	19"	22"
28"	28"	20"

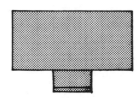

DESK

WIDTH	DEPTH	HEIGHT
50"	21"	30"
50"	22"	30"
55"	26"	29"
60"	30"	29"
72"	36"	29"

BUNCHING TABLE

WIDTH	DEPTH	HEIGHT
20"	20"	15"
19"	19"	15"
21"	21"	16"

OTTOMAN

WIDTH	DEPTH	HEIGHT
22"	18"	13"
22"	22"	16"
24"	19"	16"

SMALL ARM CHAIR

WIDTH	DEPTH	HEIGHT
18"	18"	29"
21"	22"	32"

FURNITURE TEMPLATE

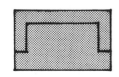

LOVE SEAT

WIDTH	DEPTH	HEIGHT
47"	28"	36"
54"	30"	36"
59"	36"	37"

ROUND COMMODE

DIAMETER	HEIGHT
18"	20"
24"	20"
26"	20"

STEP TABLE

WIDTH	DEPTH	HEIGHT
15"	27"	21"
19"	30"	21"
20"	30"	23"

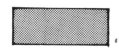

SOFA TABLE

WIDTH	DEPTH	HEIGHT
48"	16"	29"
44"	26"	30"

HEXAGONAL COMMODE

WIDTH	DEPTH	HEIGHT
27"	27"	20"
28"	28"	22"

SQUARE COMMODE

WIDTH	DEPTH	HEIGHT
24"	24"	20"
25"	25"	21"
26"	26"	20"
26"	26"	21"

SHELF UNITS

WIDTH	DEPTH	HEIGHT
17"	10"	60"
24"	10"	60"
36"	10"	36"
36"	10"	60"
48"	10"	60"

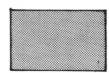

CONSOLE TELEVISION

WIDTH	DEPTH	HEIGHT
37"	17"	29"
38"	17"	29"
40"	18"	30"
45"	18"	30"
47"	19"	30"

RECTANGULAR COMMODE

WIDTH	DEPTH	HEIGHT
18"	24"	20"
22"	28"	20"

FURNITURE TEMPLATE

SERVER OR CART

LENGTH	WIDTH	HEIGHT
36"	16"	30"
52"	18"	33"
64"	16"	30"

DINING CHAIRS

WIDTH	DEPTH	HEIGHT
17"	19"	29"
20"	17"	36"
22"	19"	29"
24"	21"	31"

SEAT HEIGHT 16"

BUFFET

LENGTH	WIDTH	HEIGHT
36"	16"	31"
48"	16"	31"
52"	18"	31"

ROUND DINING TABLE

DIAMETER	HEIGHT
32"	28"
36"	28"
42"	28"
48"	28"

CHINA CABINET OR HUTCH

LENGTH	WIDTH	HEIGHT
48"	16"	65"
50"	20"	60"
62"	16"	66"

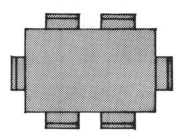

RECTANGULAR DINING TABLE

LENGTH	WIDTH	HEIGHT
42"	30"	29"
48"	30"	29"
48"	42"	29"
60"	40"	28"
60"	42"	29"
72"	36"	28"

OVAL DINING TABLE

LENGTH	WIDTH	HEIGHT
54"	42"	28"
60"	42"	28"
72"	40"	28"
72"	48"	28"
84"	42"	28"

FURNITURE TEMPLATE

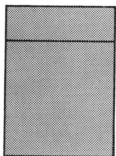

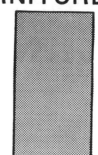

DRESSER

WIDTH	DEPTH	HEIGHT
48"	18"	30"
50"	18"	30"
52"	16"	30"
60"	18"	30"

DOUBLE BED

	LENGTH	WIDTH
Double Bed	75"	54"
	80"	54"
	84"	54"
Queen-Size Bed	80"	60"
	84"	60"
King-Size Bed	80"	72"
	80"	76"
	84"	72"
	84"	76"

SINGLE BED

	LENGTH	WIDTH
Bunk Bed	75"	30"
	75"	33"
Dormitory Bed	75"	33"
	80"	36"
Twin Bed	75"	39"
	80"	39"
	84"	39"
Three Quarter Bed	75"	48"
	80"	48"

NIGHT TABLE

LENGTH	WIDTH	HEIGHT
24"	15"	22"
22"	16"	22"
24"	18"	22"
22"	22"	22"

CHEST OF DRAWERS

WIDTH	DEPTH	HEIGHT
20"	16"	50"
26"	16"	37"
28"	15"	34"
32"	17"	43"
36"	18"	45"

DESK

WIDTH	DEPTH	HEIGHT
33"	16"	29"
36"	16"	29"
40"	20"	30"
43"	16"	30"

KITCHEN TEMPLATE

RANGE HOOD

WIDTH	HEIGHT	DEPTH
24"	5"	12"
30"	6"	17"
66"	7"	26"
72"	8"	28"

BUILT-IN COOK TOP

WIDTH	HEIGHT	DEPTH
12"	2"	18"
24"	3"	22"
48"	3"	22"

REFRIGERATOR

CU. FT.	WIDTH	HEIGHT	DEPTH
9	24"	56"	29"
12	30"	68"	30"
14	31"	63"	24"
19	34"	70"	29"
21	36"	66"	29"

SINGLE COMPARTMENT SINK

WIDTH	DEPTH
24"	21"
30"	20"

DOUBLE COMPARTMENT SINK

WIDTH	DEPTH
32"	21"
36"	20"
42"	21"

STANDARD FREE-STANDING RANGE

WIDTH	HEIGHT	DEPTH
20"	30"	24"
21"	36"	25"
30"	36"	26"
40"	36"	27"

DROP IN RANGE

WIDTH	HEIGHT	DEPTH
23"	23"	22"
24"	23"	22"
30"	24"	25"

OFFICE SEATING TEMPLATE

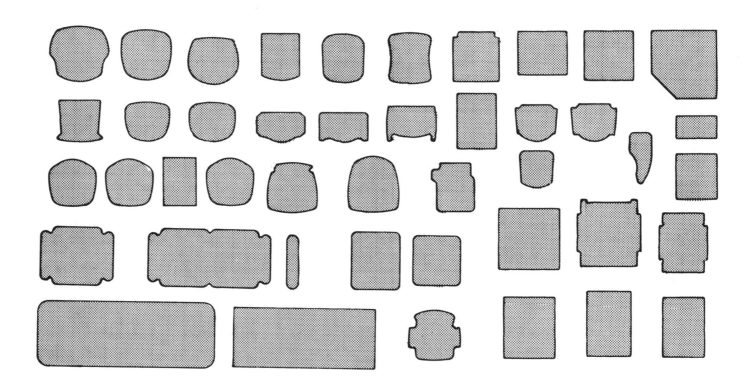

SCALE 1/4"-1 0"

OFFICE FURNITURE TEMPLATE

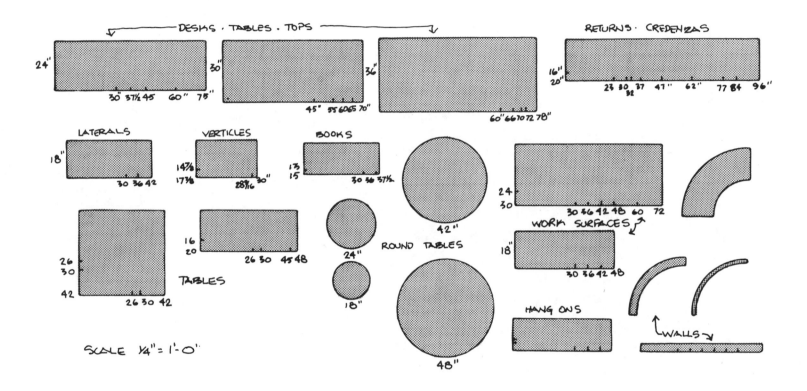

DESKS · TABLES · TOPS

RETURNS · CREDENZAS

24"   30"   36"

30 37½ 45   60" 75"

45" 55 60 65 70"

60" 66 70 72 78"

16"
20"   23 30 37   47"   62"   77 84   96"
          32

LATERALS   VERTICLES   BOOKS

18"   14⅞   13
               17⅜   15

30 36 42   28⅟₁₆ 30"   30 36 37½

42"

24
30   30 36 42 48 60   72

WORK SURFACES

16   ROUND TABLES   18"
20

26   24"   30 36 42 48
30   26 30 45 48
42
       26 30 42   18"   HANG ONS

TABLES   WALLS

SCALE ¼" = 1'-0"   48"

RESTAURANT FURNITURE TEMPLATE

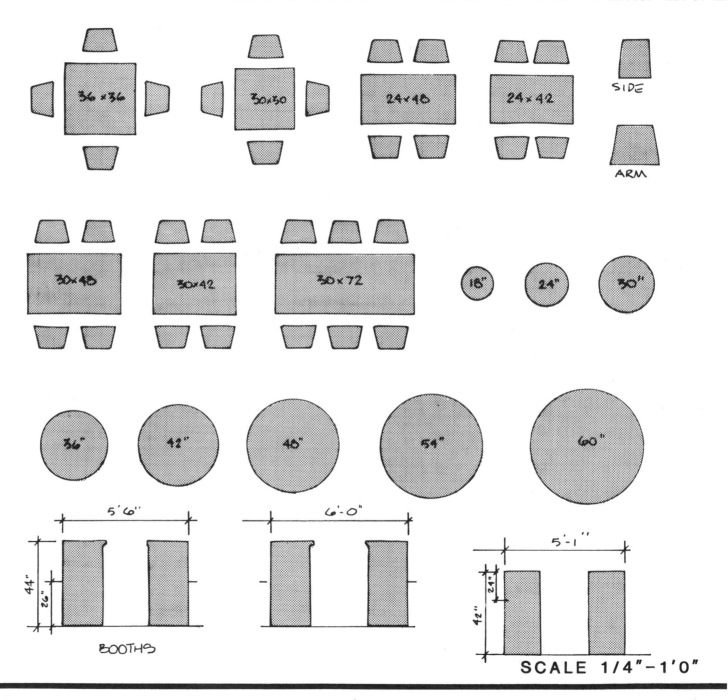

SIDE

ARM

36x36 30x30 24x46 24x42

30x48 30x42 30x72 16" 24" 30"

36" 42" 48" 54" 60"

5'6" 6'0" 5'1"

44" 42" 24"

BOOTHS

SCALE 1/4"=1'0"

ELECTRICAL SYMBOLS

Symbol	Name	Symbol	Name	Symbol	Name
	CEILING OUTLET FIXTURE		SINGLE RECEPTACLE OUTLET		SINGLE-POLE SWITCH
	RECESSED OUTLET FIXTURE		DUPLEX RECEPTACLE OUTLET		DOUBLE-POLE SWITCH
	DROP CORD FIXTURE		TRIPLEX RECEPTACLE OUTLET		THREE-WAY SWITCH
	FAN HANGER OUTLET		QUADRUPLEX RECEPTACLE OUTLET		FOUR-WAY SWITCH
	JUNCTION BOX		SPLIT-WIRED DUPLEX RECEPTACLE OUTLET		WEATHERPROOF SWITCH
	FLUORESCENT FIXTURE		SPECIAL PURPOSE SINGLE RECEPTACLE OUTLET		LOW VOLTAGE SWITCH
	TELEPHONE		230 VOLT OUTLET		PUSH-BUTTON
	INTERCOM		WEATHERPROOF DUPLEX OUTLET		CHIMES
	CEILING FIXTURE WITH PULL SWITCH		DUPLEX RECEPTACLE WITH SWITCH		TELEVISION ANTENNA OUTLET
	SPECIAL FIXTURE OUTLET		SPECIAL DUPLEX OUTLET		DIMMER SWITCH
	THERMOSTAT		FLUSH MOUNTED PANEL BOX		SPECIAL SWITCH

PLUMBING SYMBOLS

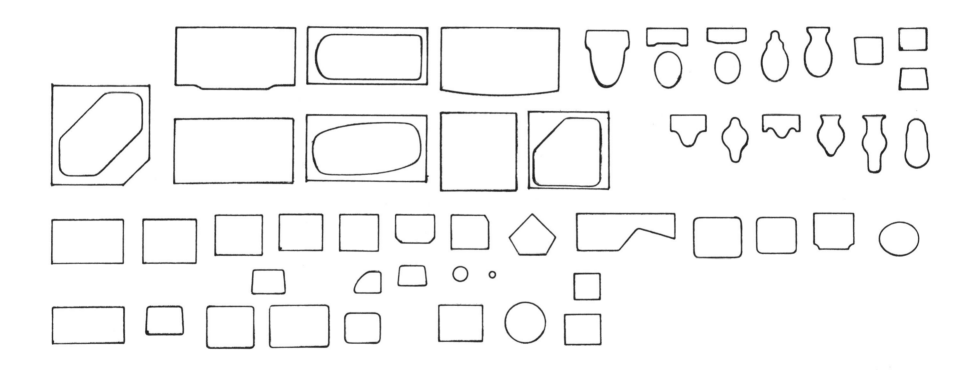

ARCHITECTURAL SYMBOLS

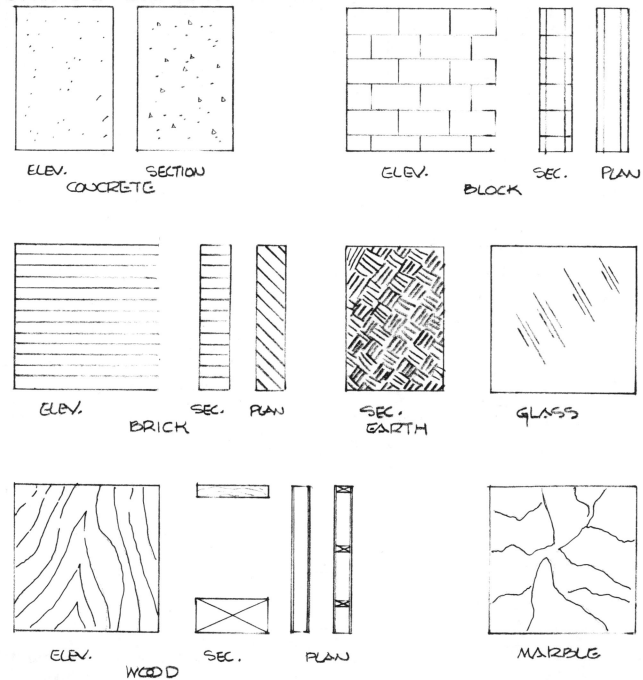

ELEV.   SECTION

CONCRETE

ELEV.   SEC.   PLAN

BLOCK

ELEV.   SEC.   PLAN

BRICK

SEC.
EARTH

GLASS

ELEV.   SEC.   PLAN

WOOD

MARBLE

JOB NAME

LOCATION

DATE

RESIDENTIAL WINDOW REPLACEMENT
FIELD MEASUREMENT GUIDE
for Wood Frame and Brick Veneer Construction

Existing exterior:

_____ Good; not to be disturbed.

_____ New siding to be installed.

_____ New siding recently installed.

_____ Brick veneer.

*If exterior wood trim is to be covered, give trim width dimensions in column F below.

Existing interior:

_____ Good; not to be disturbed.

_____ To be remodeled.

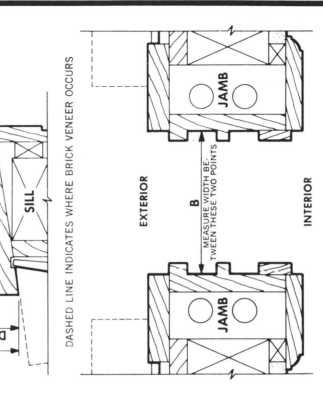

HEAD

EXTERIOR   INTERIOR

MEASURE HEIGHT BE-
TWEEN THESE TWO POINTS

A

SILL

C

D

JAMB

EXTERIOR

B

MEASURE WIDTH BE-
TWEEN THESE TWO POINTS

JAMB

INTERIOR

DASHED LINE INDICATES WHERE BRICK VENEER OCCURS

E

MULLION

LOCATION	A	B	C	D	E	F*	QTY.	PELLA UNIT SIZE	PRICE

ROLSCREEN COMPANY • PELLA, IOWA 50219

AS19-479

WINDOW SYMBOLS

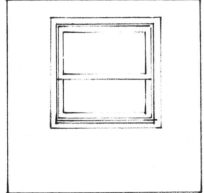

DOUBLE HUNG

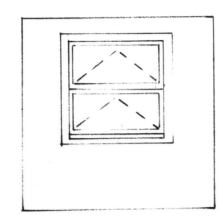

AWNING

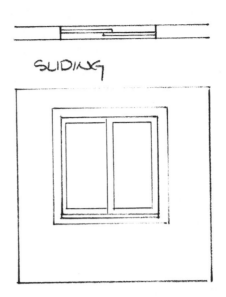

SLIDING

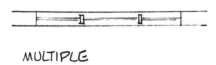

IN MASONRY

MULTIPLE

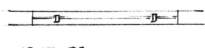

PICTURE

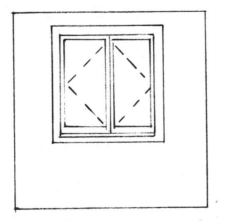

CASEMENT

Pella WOOD DOUBLE-HUNG WINDOWS

Scale 3" = 1' 0" (1:4)

FRAME — DRYWALL

¾" (19) Sheathing   ½" (13) Drywall

2 x 6 FRAME — DRYWALL

¾" (19) Sheathing   ½" (13) Drywall

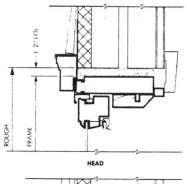

HEAD

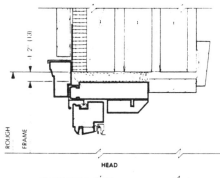

HEAD

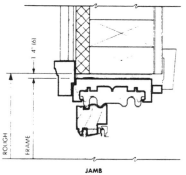

JAMB

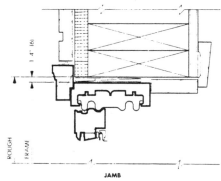

JAMB

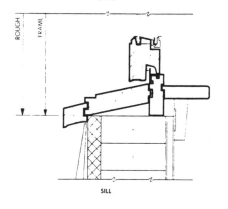

SILL

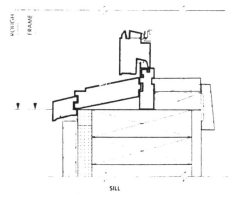

SILL

DOOR SYMBOLS

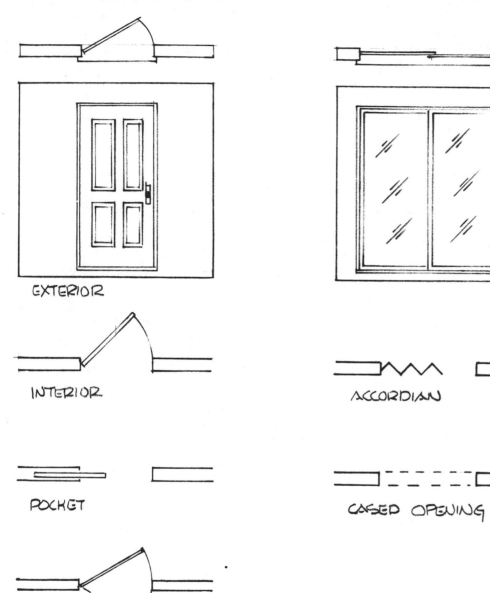

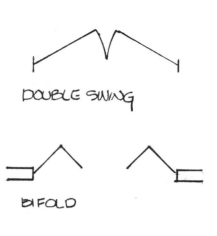

DOUBLE SWING

BIFOLD

EXTERIOR

INTERIOR

POCKET

SWING

ACCORDIAN

CASED OPENING

Pella WOOD SLIDING GLASS DOORS

Scale 3″ = 1′ 0″ (1:4)

FRAME — DRYWALL

2 x 6 FRAME — DRYWALL

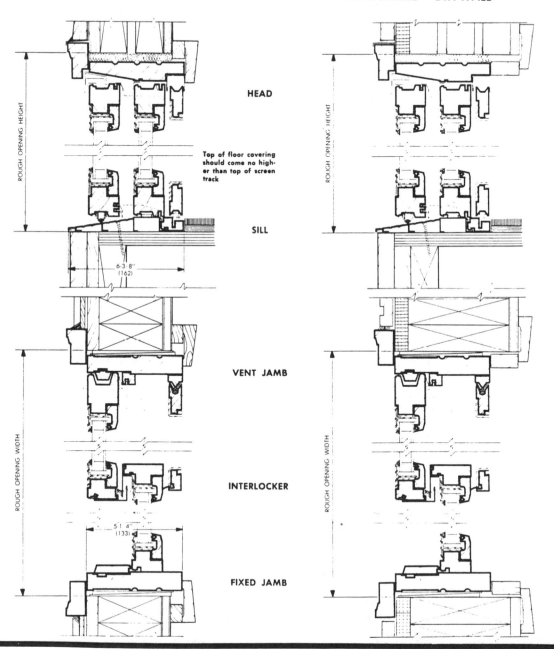

ROUGH OPENING HEIGHT

HEAD

Top of floor covering should come no higher than top of screen track

SILL

6-3/8″ (162)

VENT JAMB

ROUGH OPENING WIDTH

INTERLOCKER

5-1/4″ (133)

FIXED JAMB

ROUGH OPENING HEIGHT

ROUGH OPENING WIDTH

TECHNIQUES

In architectural drafting the line is the primary symbol used to convey space, shape, even texture. Scale and relationship are communicated by placement and dominance of lines. Lines also have certain symbolic qualities expressed in line types. Line quality communicates clarity and professionalism.

When drafting, always know what a line represents. Draw enough, but no more than necessary, to convey your meaning. Knowing and communicating clearly the construction of a cabinet is far more important than line quality, but that too is important. Make sure corners connect and that all lines are logical and contiguous with meaning.

Most architectural drafting is done on paper with pencil, but ink and plastic film also have their uses. We will, however, concentrate on pencil drawn on paper because of its flexibility and correctability.

A good set of tools will work for your drafting quality. A drafting board larger than the paper you propose to use is important. A drafting board 28" x 42" is a good architectural size, allowing the use of 24" x 36" paper. A good plastic surface for the drafting board is best. A parallel straight edge is much better than a t-square, and is more suitable for drawing long, straight lines in architectural drafting. An adjustable triangle, a drafting pencil and sharpener, a scale rule, and an eraser round out the list of basic tools. These and other items are covered in the tool section of this book.

Mount your paper, usually Clear Print or other architectural drafting vellum, to the board. Align the paper edge with the parallel bar. This will assure the accuracy of the lines and expedite removing and repositioning the paper as you work on it. Tape the paper to the board only at the corners, using drafting tape which will allow the paper to stretch without bubbling.

MAJOR LINES, the outer major elements of a plan, elevation or section, or cut lines should be the boldest. HB or F lead is indicated.

SECONDARY LINES are for internal and subordinate lines, including dimension lines. These should be as dark as major lines, but not _quite_ as dominant. HB or F lead is also good for these lines.

LAYOUT LINES are faint and may be done with F lead or a harder grade. These lines are intended to be unseen or faintly seen. This line weight is also indicated for lettering guides.

LINE TYPES:

——————————————————— Solid line for major and secondary elements

— — — — — — — — — — — Dashed line for elements above and below cut lines of plan

— . — . — . — . — . — . — Center lines

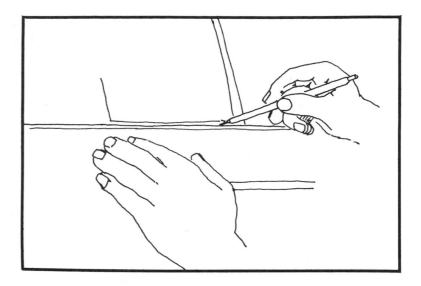

Always draw over the t-square and triangle and other tool edges, not into them. There should be a slight gap between the lead tip and the plastic tool edge. This protects the tool edge, makes it easier to see the line and reduces smudging. Pull the pencil rather than pushing it, as this keeps the paper from snagging.

Keep the lead sharp. About every 12" to 18" of line drawn will require you to sharpen. As dark a line as you can make is the one to aim for at the beginning, but thin and not fuzzy.

To help assure the evenness of a drafting line, rotate the pencil while drawing.

Make your corners clean. Avoid double lines when drawing on existing lines. If this occurs, erase both and redraw them. All lines should start and end with clarity and definition. Don't let lines fade away.

LETTERING

There is no single element more important in interior architectural drafting than lettering. This element makes the most difference in the professional look of plans and details. There are many styles of lettering and many mechanical aids for lettering, but for most notes, dimensions and details, there is <u>no substitute</u> for freehand lettering.

For large scale titles and formal presentation boards, Paratype, Kroy Lettering templates, Leroy Machines and others are acceptable. See the tool section for information on these systems.

Lettering should be neat and in scale with the drawings it is illuminating. You must train your eye along good design principles as well as your hand. A sharp pencil and the lettering guide are used to make light consistent guide lines to letter within. If you have trouble getting the lines light enough with the "F" lead, use a 2H or 4H lead for the guidelines <u>only</u>. The resultant guidelines are left on the drawing and become part of the texture Very little of the guidelines will show through when tracings are blueprinted.

A 2" or 3" triangle can be useful in judging the consistency of the vertical lines of your letters. It need not be used to draw against. Its use is to guide the eye.

It will take a great deal of time and practice to develop a good lettering style. Look at others' work and strive for consistent quality and letter shapes.

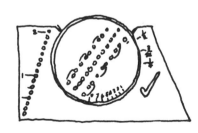

Lettering is different than "printing in that you go slowly and "draw" each letter individually.   The aesthetic of the lettered page is as important as clarity and legibility.   It is better not to begin with anything too fancy.   Instead, copy good examples of architectural lettering.   You want to develop a style but not look <u>too</u> far out.   <u>Always</u> use 2 or 3 guide lines for your lettering (and numbers) <u>every time</u> you letter on a plan.   The guide lines should be <u>lightly</u> scribed and need not be erased.   They contribute to the accepted texture of an architectural plan and, if lightly done, won't usually show up on a blue print.   I have provided a page of typical lettering styles for you to experiment with, and there are many other examples represented in plates in this book.   I have also provided a typical practice sheet for you to reproduce and use for practice.   The guide lines should be very light so they do not trick the eye.   Always practice with your drafting pencil as pens and other instruments give false practice.

LETTERING EXAMPLES

ABCDEFGHIJKLMNOPQRSTUVWXYZ 0123456789

ABCDEFGHIJKLMNOPQRSTUVWXYZ 0123456789

ABCDEFGHIJKLMNOPQRSTUVWXYZ

ABCDEFGHIJKLMNOPQRSTUVWXYZ

ABCDEFGHIJKLMNOPQRSTUVWXYZ

LETTERING PRACTICE SHEET

PLANS

The plan is a birds-eye view of an object. In the case of an architectural plan, the building is viewed as if it has been sliced in two horizontally, about three or four feet above the floor. This view with the roof removed shows all the window and door openings and interior walls.

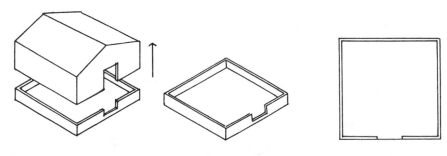

A site plan is an architectural birds-eye view with the roof on and depicts the yard, ground, parking, etc. Interior design plans usually show furniture, rugs, and other objects resting on the floor. Other specialized plan views include: electrical and plumbing; reflected ceiling; mechanical; etc.

There are various stages in the development of an architectural plan. First is the <u>sketch</u> or <u>schematic</u>. Usually a freehand drawing, this is where the idea is hatched and many sketches are discarded before the designer moves on to the next phase.

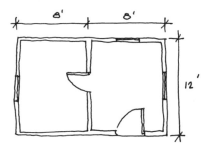

The <u>preliminary design plan</u> follows the sketch and is a drafted plan but without all the details and dimensions.

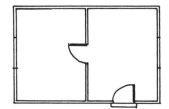

Then comes the presentation plan. This is often rendered to show texture and materials and is often colored with pencils and/or other markers. This is for a formal client presentation to gain approval for the designer to continue into the working drawing stage.

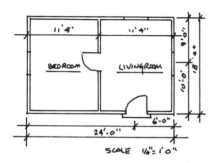

This final version of the plan gives all the information, in combination with elevations and details such as sections, that the contractor or carpenters need to construct or install the building or interior design <u>exactly</u> the way the designer and the owner wish.

Often the presentation phase is left out, and sometimes this phase is as far as a design gets. All three are related in a developmental sequence from idea to actuality.

<u>Sketch</u> or <u>schematic</u> plans are best worked out to scale rather than by eye because at small scales like 1/4" or 1/8" it is very easy to be fooled by a fraction of an inch. This can be drawn quickly, however, with pencil or felt-tip pen on inexpensive roll tracing paper. The designer can then make overlay tracing after tracing to refine and develop the design idea before drafting a more rigid and time-consuming <u>preliminary</u>. Quickness should be emphasized--but remember scale. <u>Never</u> stop with the first sketch, even though you might come back to it in the end. The more ideas you try, the better the design. In interior design plans where the walls are fixed by others, the designer can cut paper shapes to scale to represent furniture and move them about until the final solution is selected.

The preliminary should be drafted just as if it is going to be the final working drawing but stopped short of all the dimensions and details. At this stage designers often have a blueprint company make an ozalid "sepia" on tracing velum that can be used for the presentation plan, reserving the original tracing to be completed into working drawings. At this stage the plan goes in two directions: first, the formal presentation sketch and second, the working drawing. Both are similar but different in style and use of symbols.

The working plan should contain every dimension and detail that a contractor or tradesperson might ask for on the job and it should be with great accuracy. This prevents mistakes, many phone calls to the designer, and law suits from dissatisfied clients. The drawings should be as neat, organized and uncluttered as possible, and at the same time complete.

Dimensions should be drawn from the center of objects and walls to the center of other reference points when you want to show overall size and layout. Furniture and other objects are dimensioned from the outside edges to the outside edges. Exterior walls of buildings are also dimensioned from the outside edges. When a dimension line is drawn from an exterior wall to an interior wall it should be from the outside of the exterior to the center of the interior wall. This method of sizing walls and objects from the center does not depend on knowing exactly the thickness of panels, plaster, etc., when the building is laid out or designed, and therefore is simpler and more accurate with fewer measurements.

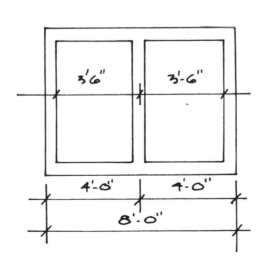

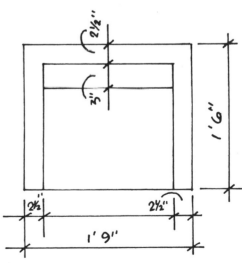

STEP BY STEP PLAN

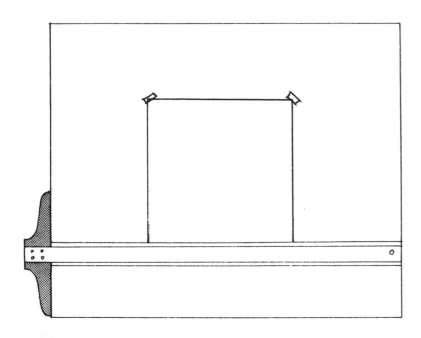

1. Square paper and tape to board.

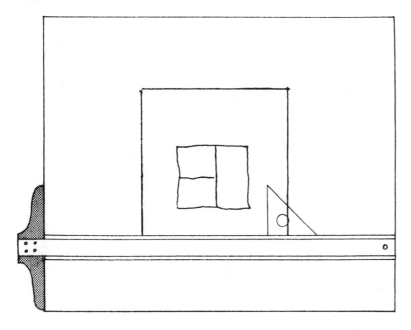

2. Rough out general dimensions of plan so it is balanced well on the page.

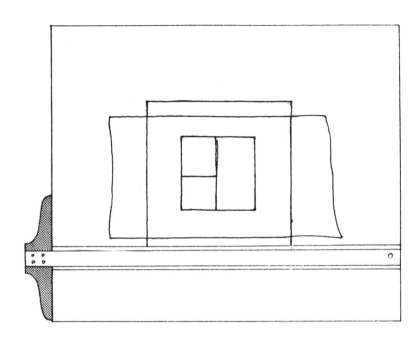

3. Use canary or other inexpensive tracing overlay until final plan is devised.

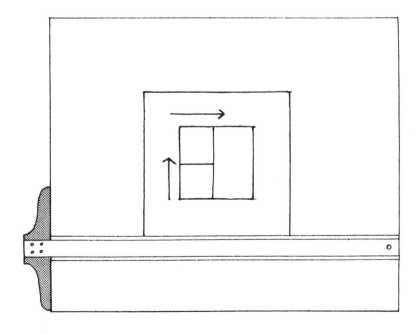

4. (Draw lightly) Draw all exterior dimensions of plan. Start in one corner and work systematically around plan.

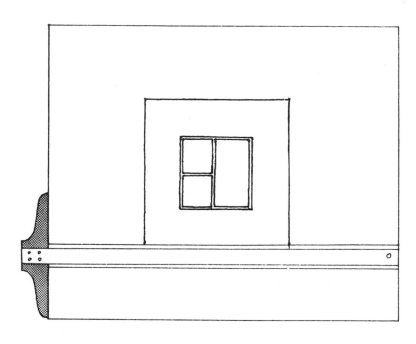

5. (Draw lightly) Add wall thicknesses and interior walls. Work outside to inside in all directions.

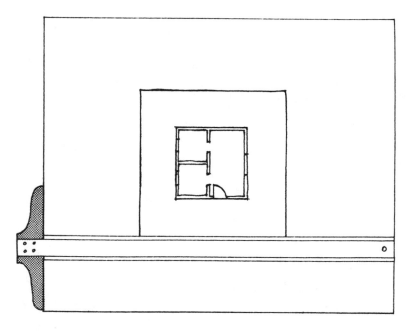

6. (Draw lightly) Check all door and window openings.

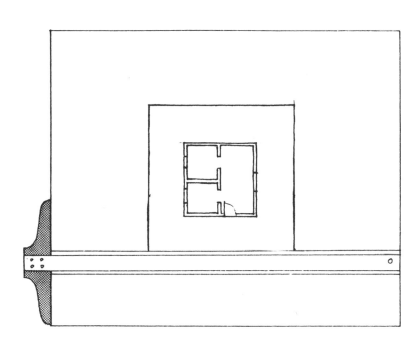

7. (Heavy lines) Darken and finalize lines. Erase construction lines and mistakes.

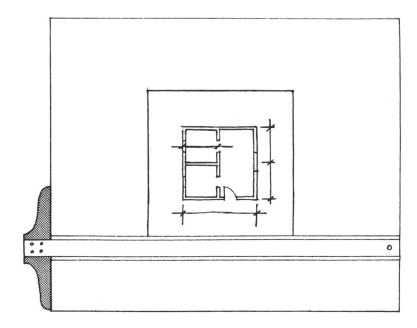

8. Add details such as furniture, texture, dimension lines, etc.   For working or presentation drawings.

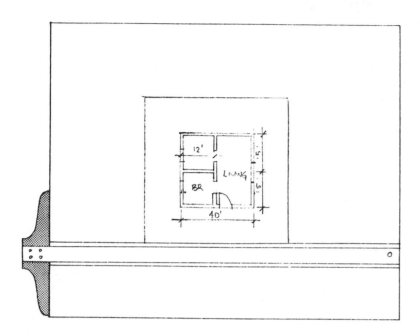

9. <u>Finally</u> letter all dimensions, notes, etc.

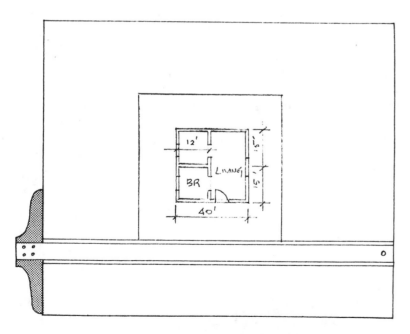

10. Clean drawing with art gum, etc.

"AS BUILT" PLAN

Often interior designers find themselves designing and remodeling existing architectural spaces. In this case the working plans for the building may not be available, or if available, they may not be accurate. The interior designer then must measure and draw up the plan from the existing building. The drafting technique in this case is the same as for any other plan, but the dimensions won't go to the center of the interior walls and the exterior of the exterior walls. Rather they will be indicated from the face of existing wall to the face of existing wall. Any new construction indicated on the same plan should revert to the same rules for new construction. The new construction should also be indicated as such on the "as built" plan.

"AS BUILT" OR MEASURED DRAWINGS

HOW TO START:

There are some basic tools that make measuring an existing space easier. They are: 1) a good sturdy legal-size yellow pad; 2) a wide 25-foot metal tape measure; 3) a #2 pencil; 4) a six-foot wooden folding rule; 5) an assistant, if possible; and 6) a ladder, if there are tall elements to measure.

The first thing you should do before you start actually measuring is to look carefully at the entire space you are measuring and, in particular, at the individual details you will need to know about when you get back to your drawing board. Don't assume you will remember how anything looks as there are always so many details that they eventually run together in memory.

After you have thoroughly looked and planned your approach, take your yellow pad and sketch every area you are to measure in a plan view. Include every detail you will measure. Give yourself enough room for dimensions and notes. You may need a sheet for each room and extras for windows, cabinets and special elements such as fireplaces and stairs. You should also have an overall sketch that at least shows how everything fits together.

When you have completed your notes, it is time to start measuring. Measure the perimeter of each room and include such details as door and window moulding widths and shapes, directions of door swings, window sizes, door and window jamb heights, odd angles, etc. Be sure to estimate wall thickness at door openings. This will help you when you piece the drawings together into a complete plan later. Note the location of any details of which you have made separate drawings so that you can key the finished drawing at your drawing board.

When you are drafting up the results of your field trip, remember that it is best to round off measurements in large areas to the nearest 1" or 1½", but that details such as mouldings should not be rounded off. You will discover that some areas don't seem to match up, especially when you start piecing several rooms together. This will require some discretion in compensating for the discrepancies. Some "fudging" of the dimensions will occur if you want to remain sane. Don't let it worry you, but if you find a lot of problems, it might be necessary to go back to the site with your tape measure and partially completed drafting to check the measurements again. It is also best to draft up the "as built" plans from your notes as soon as possible after measuring. The colder the notes, the more problems you will have.

Finally, any access to original architectural plans of a space will save much time in developing "as built" plans, even if there have been many changes in the space. A word of caution, however--don't assume the original contractor followed the plans to the inch! Check even complete plans against measurements of the actual building for accuracy. You might be surprised at the minor but significant changes you find, and at the details that didn't get into the plans that might affect your interior design intentions.

OTHER THINGS TO NOTE: Electrical outlets and switches, beam locations (make dotted lines to indicate these), ceiling height changes or details, actual door widths (for replacement doors), types of materials encountered (woods, etc.), details of cabinets, etc.

A Polaroid or 35mm camera is extremely valuable for documenting as much as possible about the space for your design files.

"AS BUILT" PLAN

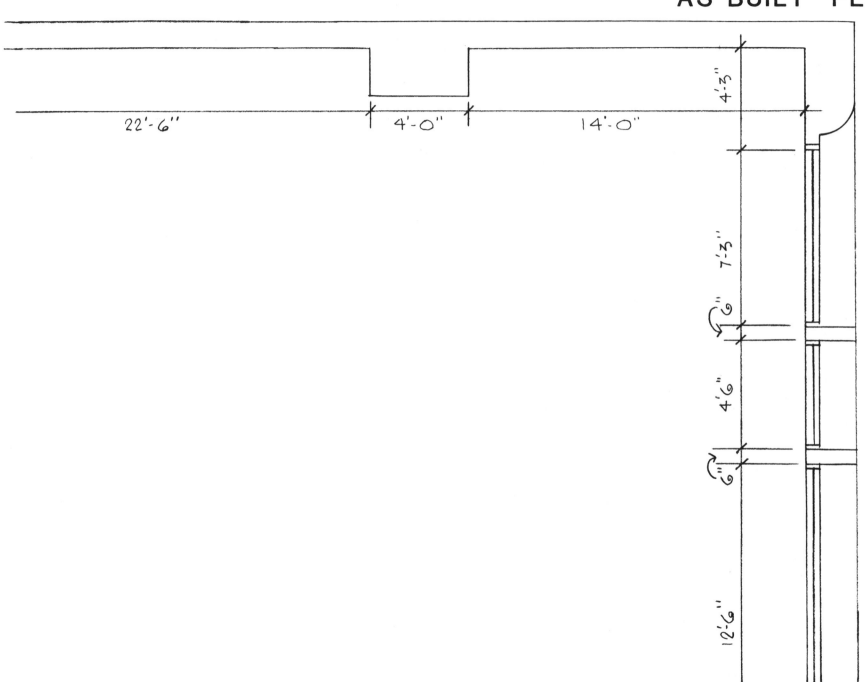

WORKING PLAN

The Working Plan or Construction Drawing represents all the basic horizontal layout information and dimensions needed by the contractors or trades people to build the design.

The graphics in this plan must be accurate and consistent. All the dimensions should be consistent and double-checked before they are transmitted to the contractor. The line quality has a great bearing both on the communication of the design and on the image of professionalism they project.

Remember that you are drawing a tracing that will be Diazo-prited for distribution and that both quality tracing paper and good, dark, clear lines are demanded.

WORKING PLAN

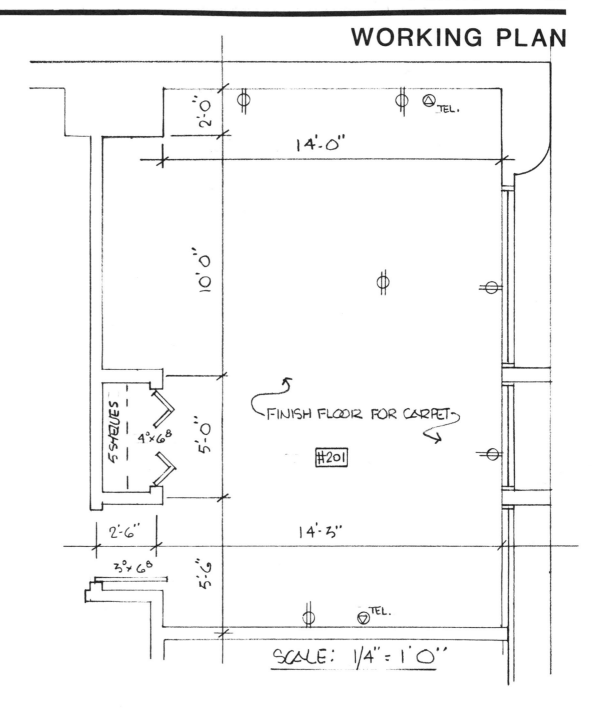

2'-0"

14'-0"

10'-0"

5 SHELVES

4⁰ × 6⁸

FINISH FLOOR FOR CARPET

#201

5'-0"

2'-6"

14'-3"

3⁰ × 6⁸

5'-6"

TEL.

TEL.

SCALE: 1/4" = 1'-0"

PRESENTATION PLAN

The Presentation Plan is often an early layout of the walls and furniture elements in a design project to show to the client for approval of the design concept. It is important that the Presentation Plan be clear and succinct. It is usually textured and rendered with wood grain and other details to give it life and make it easy for a non-professional to read. This is one of the few times that ink drawing may be indicated in interior design drafting. Often a blue, brown or black line Diazo print is made of the plans and drawing, then mounted on illustration board and colored with markers or pencils. The original is usually kept in the office as are design tracings and tracings of working drawings.

PRESENTATION PLAN

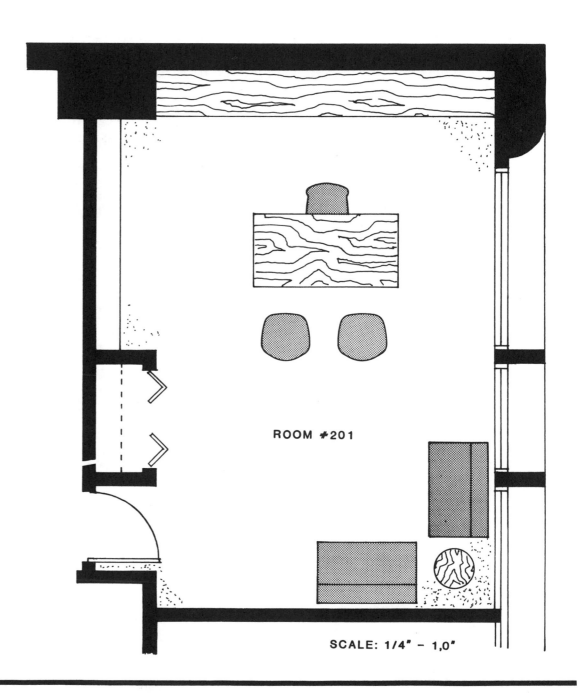

ROOM #201

SCALE: 1/4" – 1.0"

FURNITURE PLAN

This plan differs from the Presentation Drawing in that it is not usually textured, and has clear indicators of the final placement of furniture and interior design elements.   It is clearly marked with numbers and keys to the specific furniture elements.   It is also tied into a furniture schedule or description for the installer. These may be drawn for an entire floor or room by room, depending on the scale and complexity of the project, or they may be drawn up in both formats in the same or different scales.   1/8", 1/4" and 1/2" scales are typical for furniture layouts. Templates are the easiest way to do the drawing, and both general and brand-name templates are available.   Brand-name templates are available from many furniture manufacturers, including Herman Miller, Knoll, and Steelcase.

FURNITURE PLAN

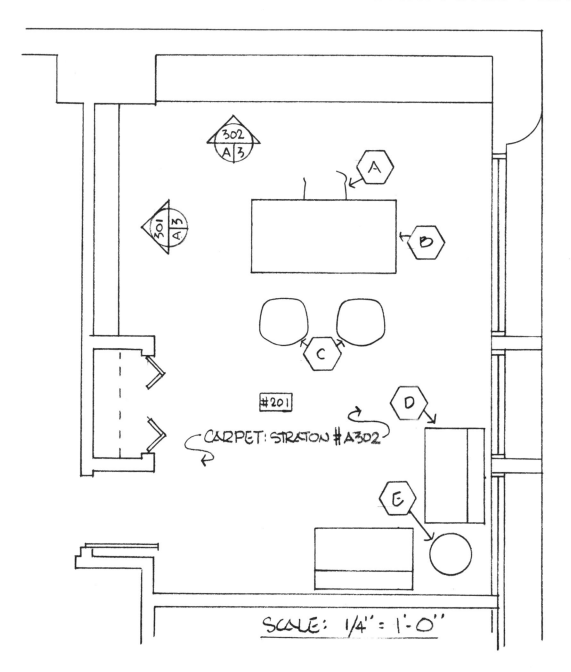

302
A|3

301
A|3

A

B

C

#201

CARPET: STRATON #A302

D

E

SCALE: 1/4" = 1'-0"

REFLECTED CEILING PLAN

A Reflected Ceiling Plan is a ceiling plan drawn as if the ceiling is reflected into a mirror on the room floor, as the drafter is looking down at the image. This allows the floor and ceiling plans to line up on the drafting board and helps coordinate all the ceiling and lighting elements with the furniture and floor elements. Sometimes the Reflected Ceiling Plan will only indicate level changes and decoration on the ceiling; sometimes only the lighting equipment; sometimes, both. Occasionally the electrical circuitry is also indicated on the Reflected Ceiling Plan, but most often there is a separate electrical plan provided by the electrical engineer. I have included examples of several types of ceiling plans as well as a symbol sheet for electrical and lighting equipment. Remember that scale is important, both to the eye and to the scale rule!

REFLECTED CEILING PLAN

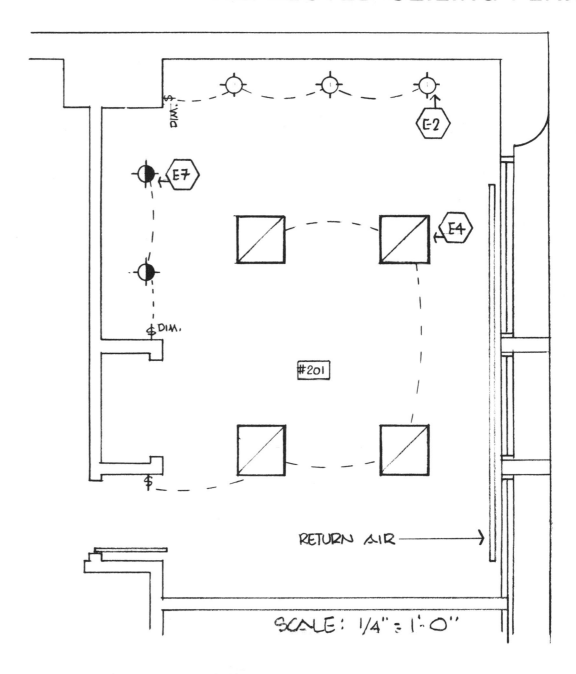

E-2

E7

E4

DIM.

DIM.

#201

RETURN AIR ⟶

SCALE: 1/4" = 1'-0"

ELEVATIONS

Elevations are merely vertical rather than horizontal "plans" of a wall or building element. The same principles apply to elevation drawing, except they rarely show cut-away elements as do plans.

ELEVATION

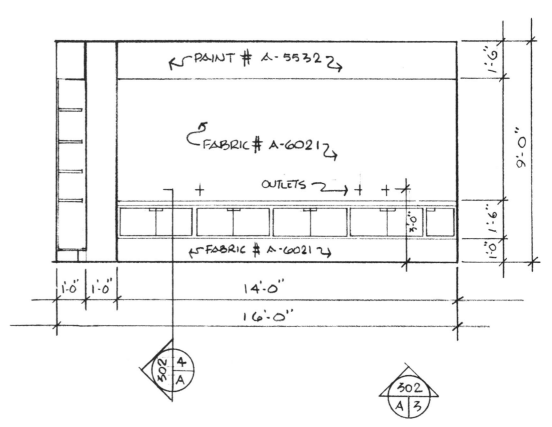

PAINT # A-5532

FABRIC # A-6021

OUTLETS

FABRIC # A-6021

1'-6"

9'-0"

1'-6"

1'-0"

3'-0"

1'-0" 1'-0"

14'-0"

16'-0"

302 / 4 / A

302 / A / 3

SCALE: 1/4" = 1'-0"

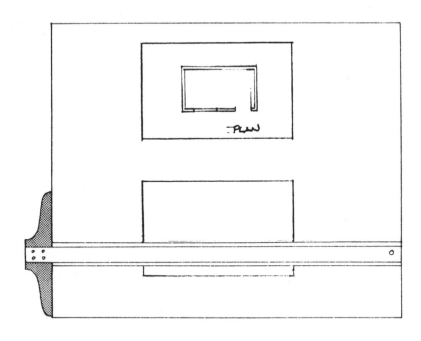

STEP BY STEP ELEVATIONS

1. Place your plan on your board above your clean sheet so that the side of the plan you wish to draw the elevation of is in line with your clean sheet.

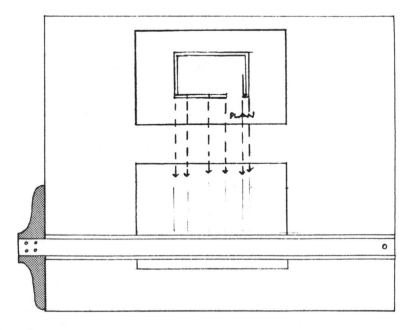

2. Drop the measurements with your triangle from the plan to the elevation sheet.

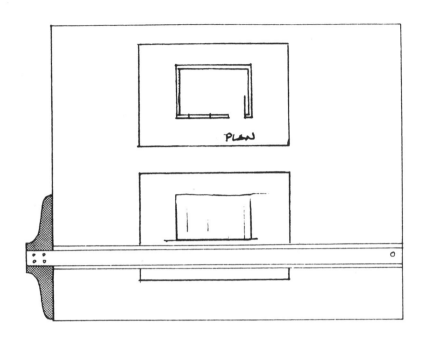

3. Establish the base line of your elevation.

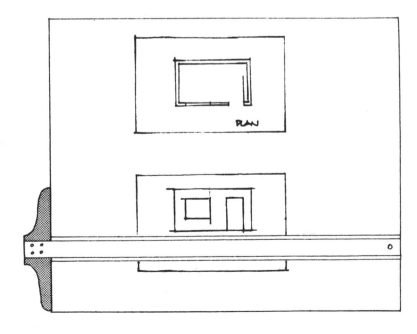

4. Measure up from the base line along the vertical lines derived from your plan to establish the sizes and locations of doors, windows, and other horizontal lines. These measurements can come from section drawings if available.

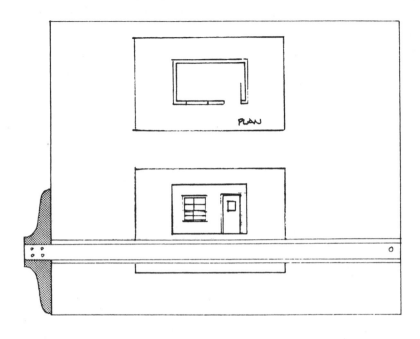

5. Clean up your construction lines.

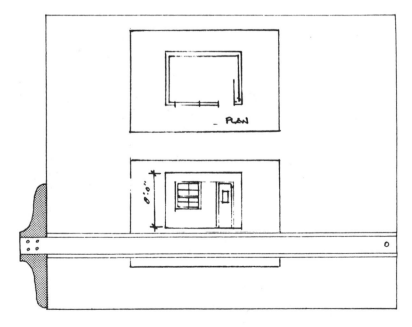

6. Put in any dimensions and notes necessary to convey the size and construction of the object.

INTERIOR ELEVATIONS

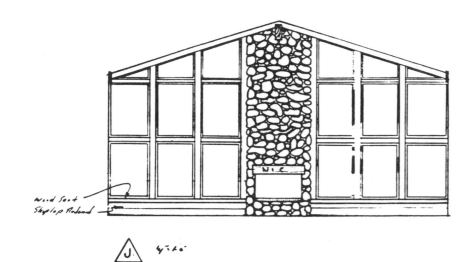

Wood Seat
Shiplap Redwood

J 4'=1'-0"

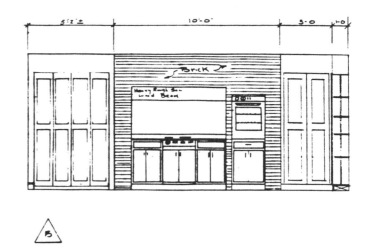

5'2"±   10'-0"   3'-0"   1'-0"

Brick

Heavy Rough Sawn
Wood Beam

B

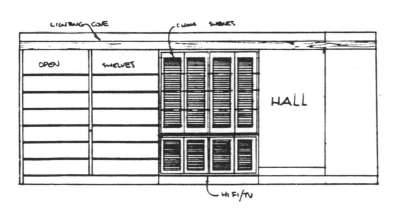

LIGHTING COVE   CHINA SHELVES

OPEN   SHELVES

HALL

HI FI/TV

G

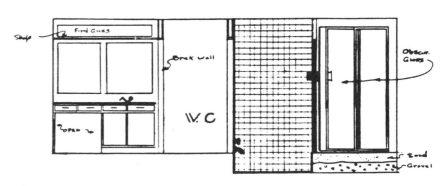

Fixed Glass   Shelf

Brick Wall

W.C   Obscure Glass

Open

Sand
Gravel

E

SECTIONS

Sections are usually vertical cutaway views that show in two dimensions the construction elements of an area of the building, furniture or construction. They use the same principles as plan and elevation but they are usually drawn at a larger scale. Often elevations and sections are combined in the same drawing for cabinets and interior elements.

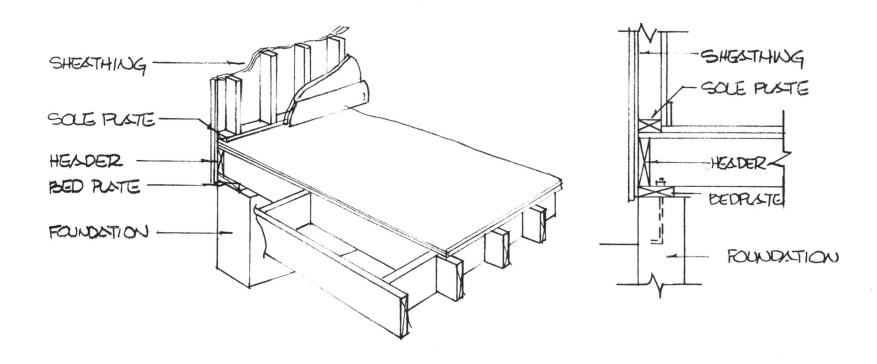

SHEATHING

SOLE PLATE

HEADER

BED PLATE

FOUNDATION

SHEATHING

SOLE PLATE

HEADER

BEDPLATE

FOUNDATION

CABINET SECTION

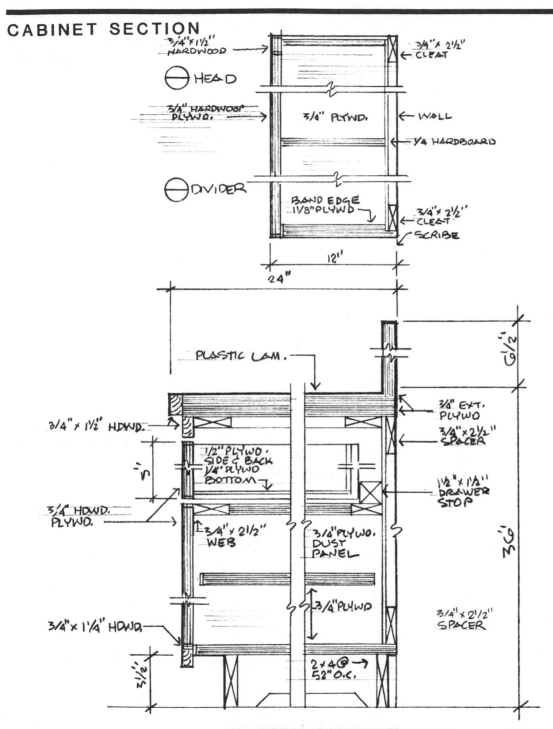

3/4" x 1 1/2" HARDWOOD

3/4" x 2 1/2" CLEAT

⊖ HEAD

3/4" HARDWOOD PLYWD.

3/4" PLYWD.

WALL

1/4 HARDBOARD

⊖ DIVIDER

BAND EDGE 1 1/8" PLYWD

3/4" x 2 1/2" CLEAT

SCRIBE

12"

24"

PLASTIC LAM.

6 1/2"

3/4" x 1 1/2" HDWD.

3/8" EXT. PLYWD

3/4" x 2 1/2" SPACER

1/2" PLYWD. SIDE & BACK
1/4" PLYWD BOTTOM

5"

1 1/2" x 1 1/2" DRAWER STOP

3/4" HDWD. PLYWD.

3/4" x 2 1/2" WEB

3/8" PLYWD. DUST PANEL

36"

3/4" PLYWD

3/4" x 1 1/4" HDWD

3/4" x 2 1/2" SPACER

5 1/2"

2 x 4 @ 52" O.C.

DETAILS

A detail is a drawing that describes exactly how a particular element of a design goes together. It also describes the material from which it is made. The plans and elevations give the general information while the detail gives the specifics. For example, the general location of cabinets would be given on the plan and on the elevation, while the detail would show the actual thickness of the wood fascia and the shape and size of the door edges and hardware.

Plans are usually drawn at 1/8", 1/4" or 1/2" scale, or in some cases even in full scale. This "magnification" allows maximum information to show. The larger the scale, the more precise the detail will be. You must judge the amount of information required by the carpenter or cabinet maker and respond accordingly.

While it is true that a great deal of information is required to make sure that your ideas are being followed by the cabinet maker or craftsperson, it is often the case that specific machines and materials are unique to a particular craftsperson or shop and it is difficult to anticipate all these variables in the design stage. It is important that the designer communicate with the craftsperson to find out his or her capabilities and requirements, and how these might affect the design. this might be done as the original drawing is prepared, or the designer might require the craftsperson to submit "shop drawings" to show the final and detailed construction that will be utilized in the project.

Because of the interface with the craftsperson over the "shop drawing" it is not necessary for the Design Details to call out every nail and screw. You need to indicate only those important details and the elements which you do not wish to leave up to the choice of the craftsperson. In other words, plans are the least specific, detail are the next, and shop drawings are the most specific.

RULES OF DETAILING

1. Be specific and accurate. Draw the object as it is built, in that sequence. Think through every place where the craftsperson might go wrong.

2. Be logical in your graphic arrangement.

3. Make all the notes and views clear and label them neatly.

4. In notes, sizes usually come first, then the name of the piece, spacing, and finally, any other information.

5. The inside of a building or element is always drawn from right to left, the outside is drawn from left to right.

6. Always use the actual size of wood and other materials in detail drawings. When you draw a 2x4 (a 2x4 actually measures $1\frac{1}{2}$x$3\frac{1}{2}$), remember that lumber is noted as it is named (nominal size, i.e. 2x4) even though it is drawn its actual size. Milled or special materials such as moulding or plywood are drawn and noted in their actual size.

7. Notes and leaders should never interfere with, but should rather enhance, the neatness and clarity of the drawings.

8. Each detail should stand alone with its own notes as much as possible.

9. Brand name materials and items should be avoided in a "bid" project though they are perfectly appropriate in a job where they are agreed upon with the client.

10. Abbreviations and slang should be avoided in notes, except in trade standard usages. Check the Architectural Graphic Standards or other sources for such abbreviations.

11. Dimension Types:

(a) A dimension written simply will be held by the craftsperson within reasonable tolerances.

(b) A dimension with "minimum" next to it may be larger but not smaller.

(c) A dimension with "maximum" next to it may be smaller but not larger.

(d) "Not to Scale" should be noted if that is the case of the drawing.

(e) "Hold" means that the dimension is highly critical and must be maintained at all cost.

(f) "Varies" means that the dimension may fluctuate.

12. Fractions should be avoided when possible, and should conform to 1/8" or 1/4" increments if used.

13. Materials should be clearly indicated in symbol form.

14. Profile drawings show that the shape and outline stand out. They also give a "3-D" effect and allow the drawing to be read more easily.

15. Reference notes and keys to the plans and elevations should always be used so that the craftsperson can see where the detail drawing occurs in the overall scheme

SUGGESTED MINIMUM REQUIREMENTS FOR ARCHITECTURAL DRAWINGS
OF CASEWORK AND PLASTIC TOPS

Elevations for conventional casework[1] should be shown on the architectural drawings as suggested below.

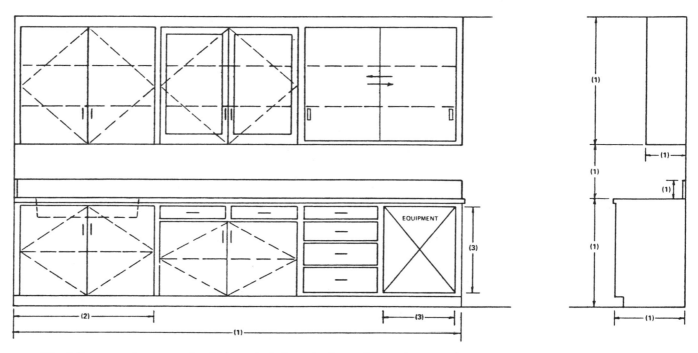

The following information should be included on the floor plan or elevations for casework:
- (1) Indicate basic overall dimensions.
- (2) Indicate dimensions of those portions which are required to be of predetermined or controlled size.
- (3) Indicate dimensions required for installation of items of equipment.
- (4) Indicate whether face frame construction or flush overlay type construction.
- (5) Indicate whether lipped or flush installation of doors and drawers if face frame construction.
- (6) Indicate whether sliding or hinged doors, including swing if hinged.
- (7) Indicate thickness of cabinet doors if other than 3/4" is required.
- (8) The only details required to be shown are those not shown in the W.I.C. Manual or those which involve installation of unusual equipment in the casework.
- (9) Note if and where locks are required.
- (10) Indicate shelves and note whether fixed or adjustable. Do not indicate thickness of shelves unless modification of W.I.C. standards is desired.
- (11) Indicate kind of top. See Sections 16 and 17 for plan requirements.

VANITY BASE STANDARDS

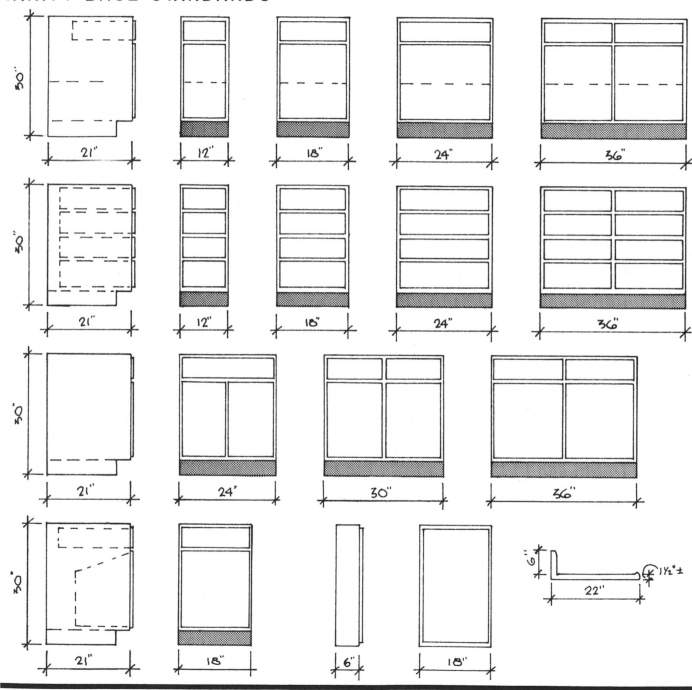

BASE CABINET STANDARDS

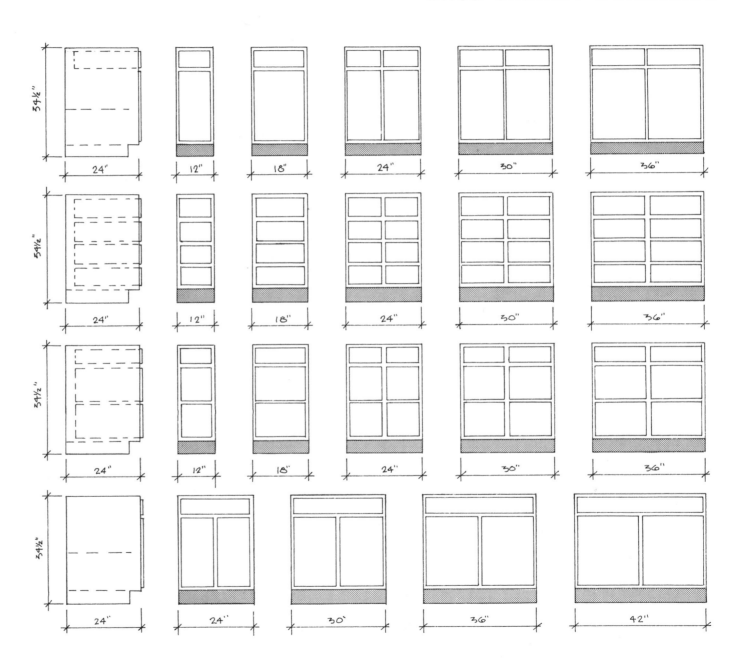

OVERHEAD CABINET STANDARDS

SUGGESTED MINIMUM SIZES FOR PARTS OF A CABINET

Face frame	3/4"
Ends and divisions	
Flush overlay	3/4"
Economy	1/2"
Custom premium	5/8"
Shelves	
Economy	
Solid stock or particleboard	3/4"
Plywood	5/8"
Custom and premium	3/4"
Length	
Over 3'-6" in length and adjustable	1"
Over 4'-0" in length and adjustable	1"
Tops and bottom	
Economy	Same as shelves
Custom and premium	3/4"
Length over 4'-0"	1"
Web members or stretcher	3/4" x 2"
Backs	
Economy untempered hardboard	1/8"
Custom and premium--Plywood or	
tempered hardboard	1/4"
Exposed backs	3/4"
Breadboards	3/4"
Drawers	
Side, sub fronts and backs	
Economy	7/16"
Custom and premium	1/2"
Bottoms	
Economy (18" maximum width)	1/8"
Economy (over 18")	1/4"
Custom and premium	1/4"
Cabinet door faces	
All grades	3/4"

Construction methods, lumber and material sizes, and dimensions of furniture and cabinets are all extremely important in developing an interior design plan. No designer can remember all this information, therefore it is important to become familiar with references and begin to collect a library of them.

Nominal Rough	Douglas Fir Hemlock Western Red Cedar		Redwood		Ponderosa Pine Sugar Pine	
	Thickness	Width	Thickness	Width	Thickness	Width
1"	$\frac{11}{16}$"		$\frac{11}{16}$"		$\frac{3}{4}$"	
1¼"	$\frac{15}{16}$"		1"		1"	
1½"	$1\frac{3}{16}$"				1¼"	
2"	$1\frac{7}{16}$"	1½"	1½"	1½"	1½"	1½"
3"	$2\frac{7}{16}$"	2½"	2½"	2½"	2½"	2½"
4"	$3\frac{7}{16}$"	3¼"	3½"	3½"	3½"	3½"
5"		4¼"		4½"		4½"
6"		5¼"		5½"		5½"
8"		7"		7¼"		7¼"
10"		9"		9¼"		9¼"
12"		11"		11¼"		11¼"
Over 12"		1" Off		¾" Off		¾" Off

Nominal Rough	Thickness	Width
1"	$\frac{3}{4}$"	
1¼"	1"	
1½"	1¼"	
2"	1½"	1½"
3"	2½"	2½"
4"	3½"	3½"
5"		4¼"
6"		5¼"
8"		7"
10"		9"
12"		11"
Over 12"		1" Off

VENEER CORE

All plies are veneer – less than ¼" thick. Middle ply is called the "center." Plies on either side of the center, but beneath the outer plies, are called "crossbandings." Outer plies are called "faces" and "backs." Thickness varies from 1/8" to ¾" or more – odd number of plies from 3 to 11 or more.

LUMBER CORE

Center ply, called the "core" is composed of strips of lumber edge-glued into a solid slab. This type is usually 5-ply, ¾" thick but other thicknesses from ½" to 1-1/8" are manufactured for special uses. There are three main core types:

a. **Staved** – all strips random length, butt-joined.

b. **Full-Length** – all strips one-piece.

c. **Banded** – outside strips full-length, others random length. Banding may be same type of lumber as rest of core but is usually a different species. Banding may include all four edges. Banded plywood is almost always produced for special uses – furniture, desk tops, and cupboard doors.

PARTICLEBOARD CORE

Medium density boards made from wood particles and called variously "chip board" "particleboard" or "shavings board" are being used more and more to replace lumber core in plywood. Developed from a need to increase the utilization of our remaining timber reserves, these boards stand on their own merits against solid lumber in all products where they are used interchangeably.

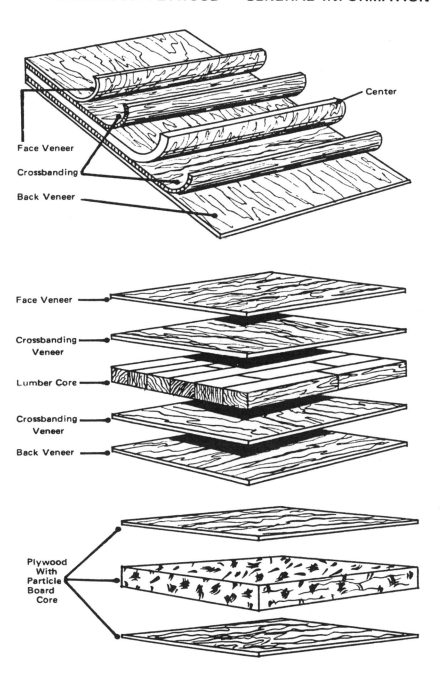

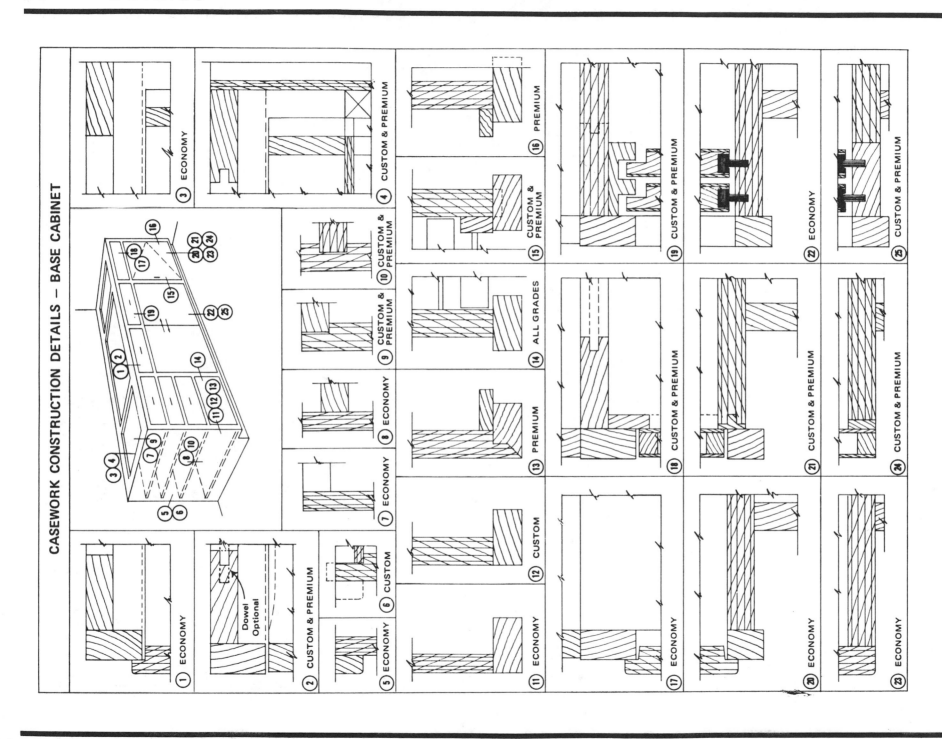

CASEWORK CONSTRUCTION DETAILS — BASE CABINET

1 ECONOMY
2 CUSTOM & PREMIUM — Dowel Optional
3 ECONOMY
4 CUSTOM & PREMIUM
5 ECONOMY
6 CUSTOM
7 ECONOMY
8 ECONOMY
9 CUSTOM & PREMIUM
10 CUSTOM & PREMIUM
11 ECONOMY
12 CUSTOM
13 PREMIUM
14 ALL GRADES
15 CUSTOM & PREMIUM
16 PREMIUM
17 ECONOMY
18 CUSTOM & PREMIUM
19 CUSTOM & PREMIUM
20 ECONOMY
21 CUSTOM & PREMIUM
22 ECONOMY
23 ECONOMY
24 CUSTOM & PREMIUM
25 CUSTOM & PREMIUM

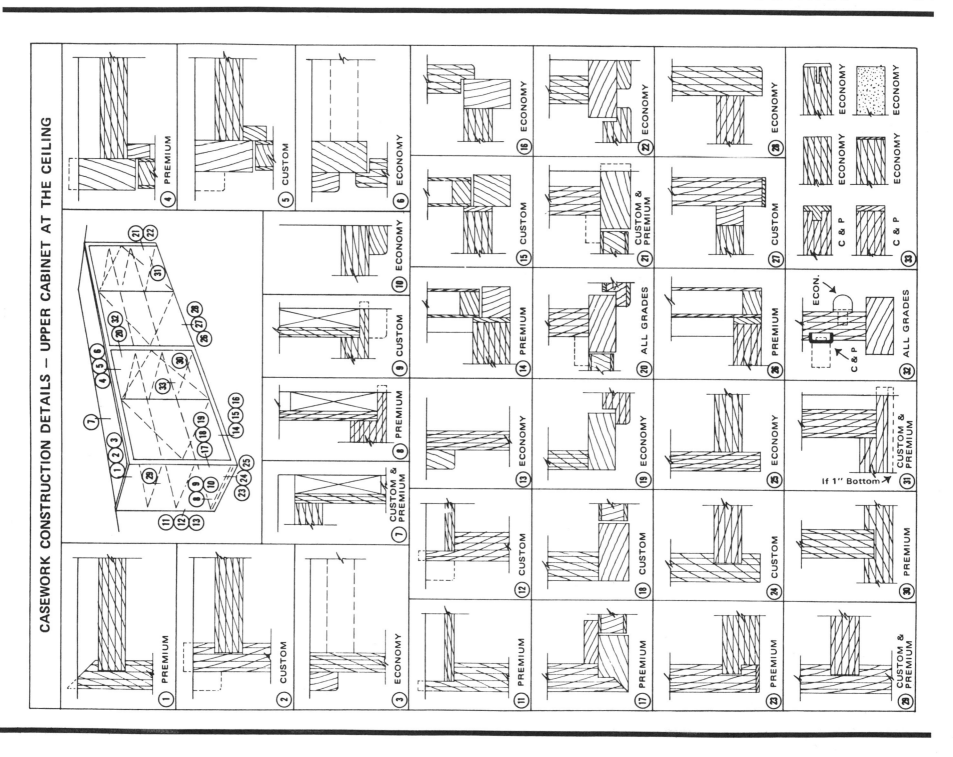

CASEWORK CONSTRUCTION DETAILS – UPPER CABINET AT THE CEILING

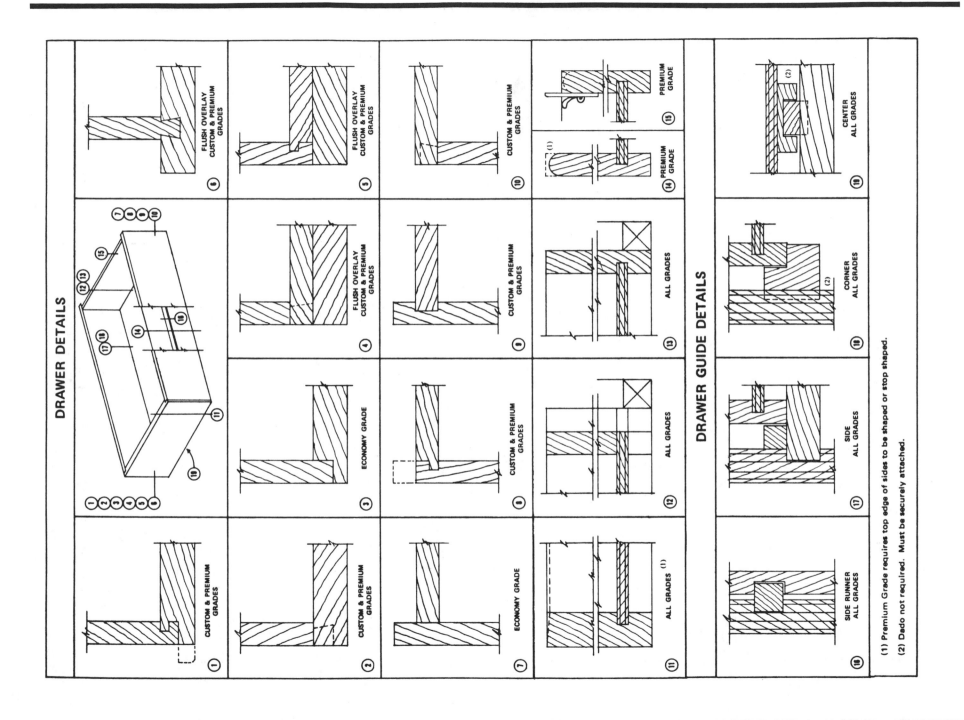

DRAWER DETAILS

1. CUSTOM & PREMIUM GRADES
2. CUSTOM & PREMIUM GRADES
3. ECONOMY GRADE
4. FLUSH OVERLAY CUSTOM & PREMIUM GRADES
5. FLUSH OVERLAY CUSTOM & PREMIUM GRADES
6. FLUSH OVERLAY CUSTOM & PREMIUM GRADES
7. ECONOMY GRADE
8. CUSTOM & PREMIUM GRADES
9. CUSTOM & PREMIUM GRADES
10. CUSTOM & PREMIUM GRADES
11. ALL GRADES (1)
12. ALL GRADES
13. ALL GRADES
14. PREMIUM GRADE
15. PREMIUM GRADE

DRAWER GUIDE DETAILS

16. SIDE RUNNER ALL GRADES
17. SIDE ALL GRADES
18. CORNER ALL GRADES
19. CENTER ALL GRADES

(1) Premium Grade requires top edge of sides to be shaped or stop shaped.

(2) Dado not required. Must be securely attached.

DEFINITIONS & DETAILS FOR PLASTIC LAMINATE TOPS

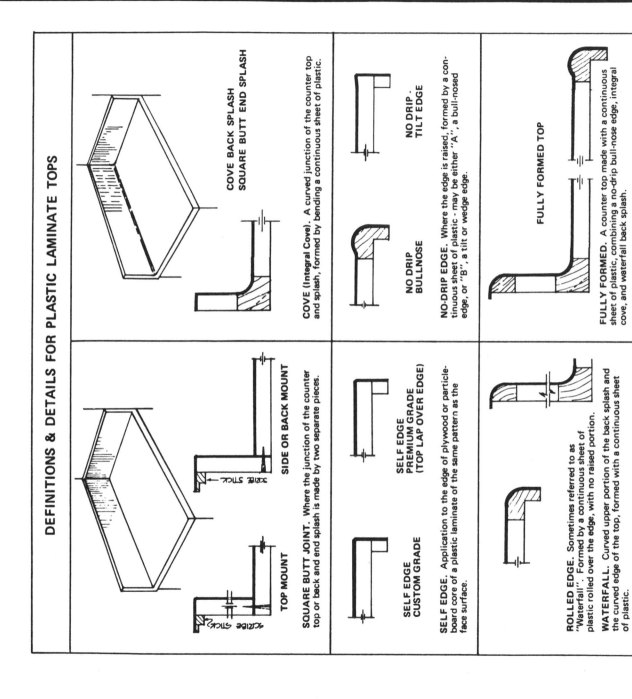

COVE BACK SPLASH
SQUARE BUTT END SPLASH

COVE (Integral Cove). A curved junction of the counter top and splash, formed by bending a continuous sheet of plastic.

SIDE OR BACK MOUNT

TOP MOUNT

SQUARE BUTT JOINT. Where the junction of the counter top or back and end splash is made by two separate pieces.

NO DRIP - TILT EDGE

NO DRIP BULLNOSE

NO-DRIP EDGE. Where the edge is raised, formed by a continuous sheet of plastic - may be either "A", a bull-nosed edge, or "B", a tilt or wedge edge.

SELF EDGE PREMIUM GRADE (TOP LAP OVER EDGE)

SELF EDGE CUSTOM GRADE

SELF EDGE. Application to the edge of plywood or particle-board core of a plastic laminate of the same pattern as the face surface.

ROLLED EDGE. Sometimes referred to as "Waterfall". Formed by a continuous sheet of plastic rolled over the edge, with no raised portion.

WATERFALL. Curved upper portion of the back splash and the curved edge of the top, formed with a continuous sheet of plastic.

FULLY FORMED TOP

FULLY FORMED. A counter top made with a continuous sheet of plastic, combining a no-drip bull-nose edge, integral cove, and waterfall back splash.

TYPES OF SINK INSTALLATIONS

Self Edge

Metal Sink Rim

TYPES OF EDGING

SNAP ON STAINLESS STEEL EDGE

FLUSH METAL OR PLASTIC TEE TYPE EDGE

TIGHT JOINT FASTENERS

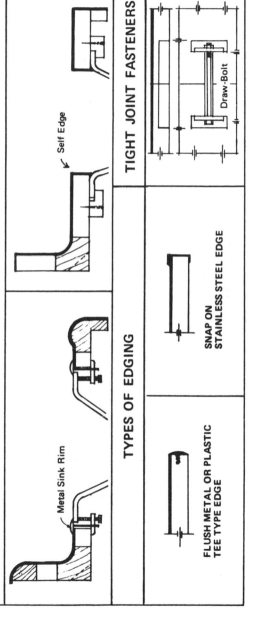

Draw-Bolt

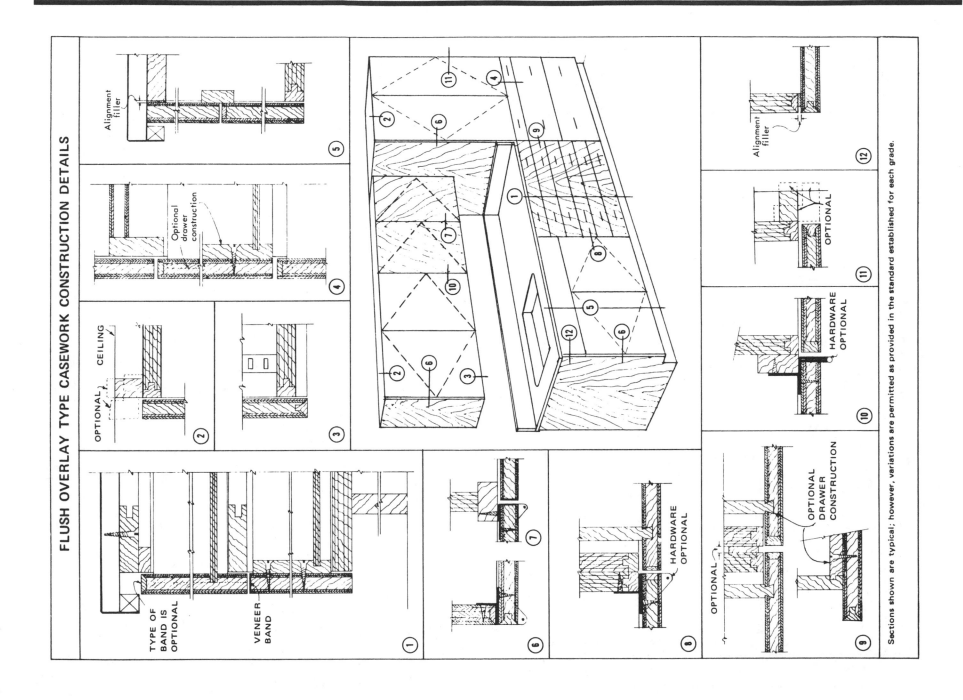

FLUSH OVERLAY TYPE CASEWORK CONSTRUCTION DETAILS

Sections shown are typical; however, variations are permitted as provided in the standard established for each grade.

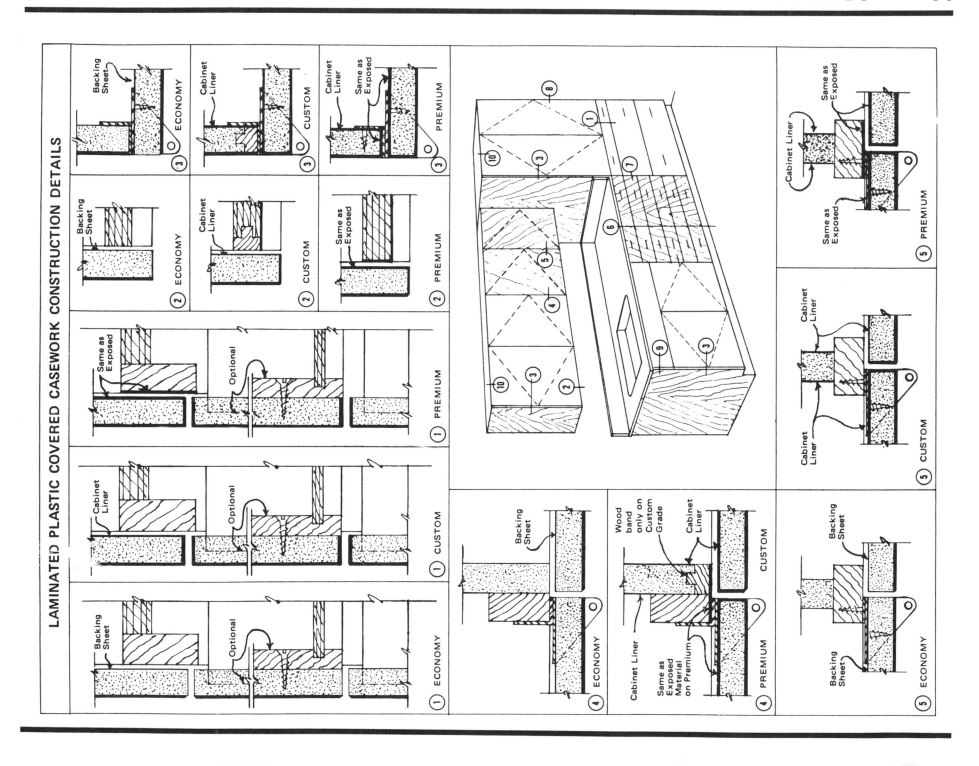

LAMINATED PLASTIC COVERED CASEWORK CONSTRUCTION DETAILS

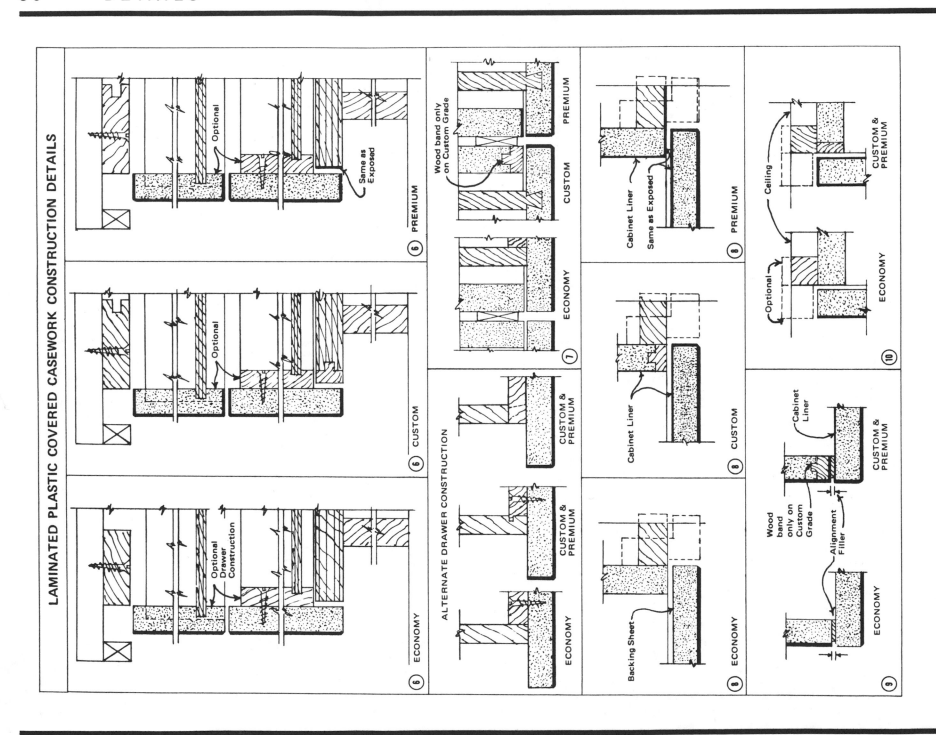

LAMINATED PLASTIC COVERED CASEWORK CONSTRUCTION DETAILS

Optional — PREMIUM ⑥

Same as Exposed

Optional — CUSTOM ⑥

Optional Drawer Construction — ECONOMY ⑥

Wood band only on Custom Grade — PREMIUM · CUSTOM ⑦

ECONOMY ⑦

ALTERNATE DRAWER CONSTRUCTION

CUSTOM & PREMIUM

CUSTOM & PREMIUM

ECONOMY

Cabinet Liner · Same as Exposed — PREMIUM ⑧

Cabinet Liner — CUSTOM ⑧

Backing Sheet — ECONOMY ⑧

Ceiling — CUSTOM & PREMIUM ⑩

Optional — ECONOMY ⑩

Wood band only on Custom Grade · Cabinet Liner · Alignment Filler — CUSTOM & PREMIUM ⑨

ECONOMY ⑨

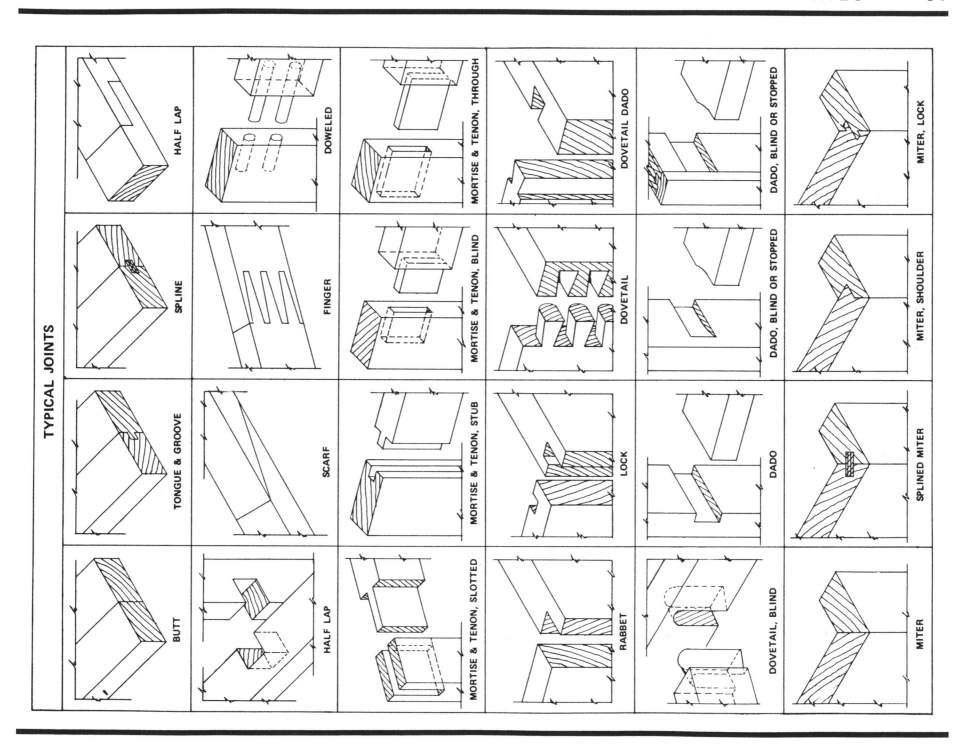

TYPICAL JOINTS

HALF LAP

DOWELED

MORTISE & TENON, THROUGH

DOVETAIL DADO

DADO, BLIND OR STOPPED

MITER, LOCK

SPLINE

FINGER

MORTISE & TENON, BLIND

DOVETAIL

DADO, BLIND OR STOPPED

MITER, SHOULDER

TONGUE & GROOVE

SCARF

MORTISE & TENON, STUB

LOCK

DADO

SPLINED MITER

BUTT

HALF LAP

MORTISE & TENON, SLOTTED

RABBET

DOVETAIL, BLIND

MITER

PROFILES OF STOCK STICKING FOR SASH AND DOORS

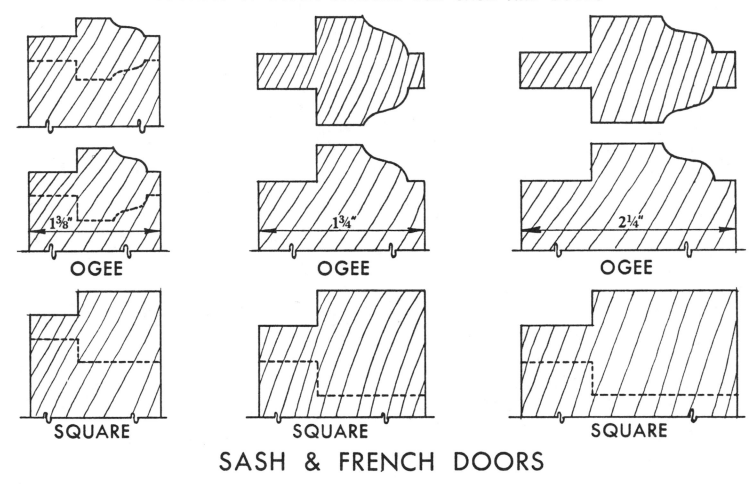

OGEE   1⅜"

OGEE   1¾"

OGEE   2¼"

SQUARE

SQUARE

SQUARE

SASH & FRENCH DOORS

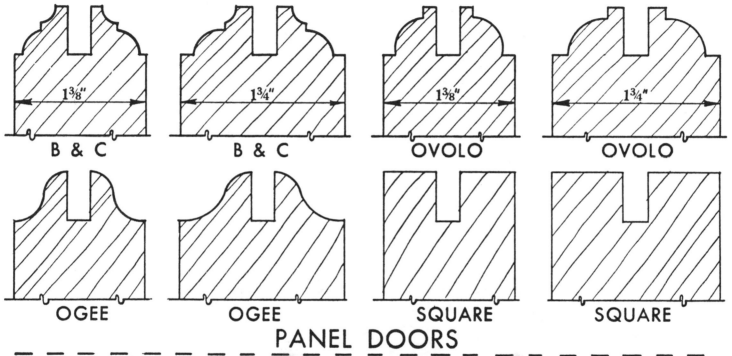

PANEL DOORS

WHEN STOCK SASH OR DOORS ARE SPECIFIED OR INDICATED THE STICKING WILL BE OPTIONAL WITH THE SUPPLIER.
SPECIAL STICKINGS FOR EITHER SASH OR DOORS INVOLVE SEVERAL SPECIAL MANUFACTURING OPERATIONS, AND ARE RELATIVELY COSTLY.

EXAMPLES

Without a doubt the best way to learn how to draft is to do it! The next best way, and part of the process of "doing it" is to follow the example of others who have come before us. This section compiles many examples of professional and student work for you to study. Use them as guides, idea stimulators, copy book examples, standards and models. Analyze them carefully, but feel free to establish your own style and methods. There are always many correct ways of solving the same problem. Your solution may blaze a new graphic trail.

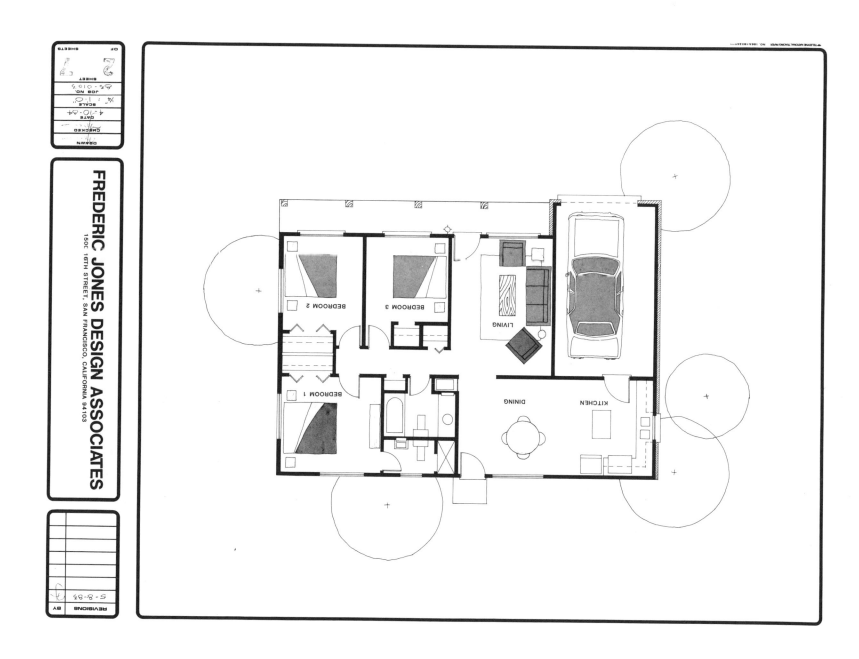

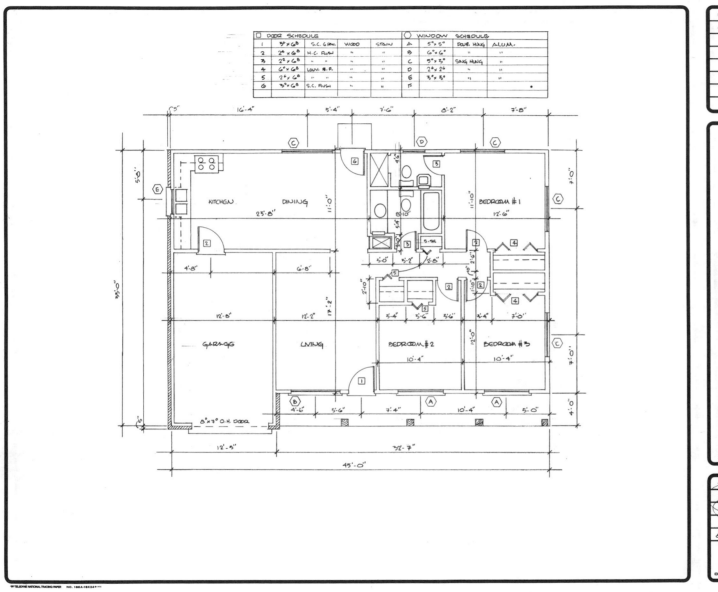

FREDERIC JONES DESIGN ASSOCIATES
1500 18TH STREET SAN FRANCISCO, CALIFORNIA 94103

REVISIONS	BY
6-2-85	

DRAWN
CHECKED
DATE 4-10-84
SCALE ¼" = 1'-0"
JOB NO. 83-0103
SHEET

3 7
OF   SHEETS

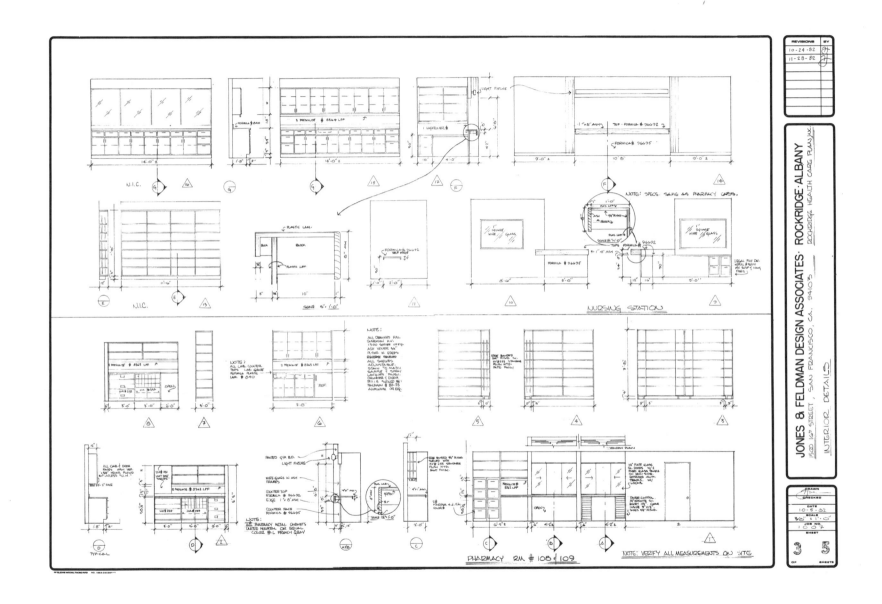

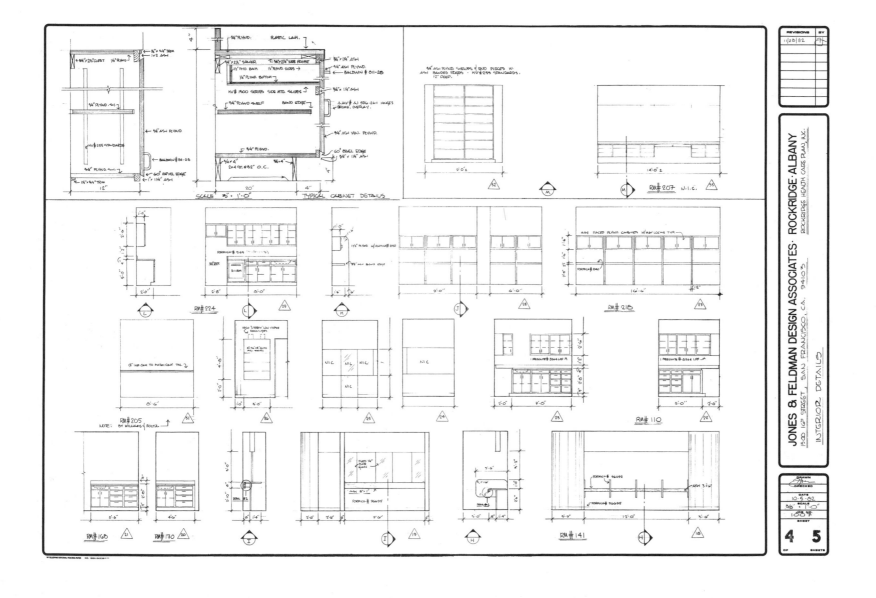

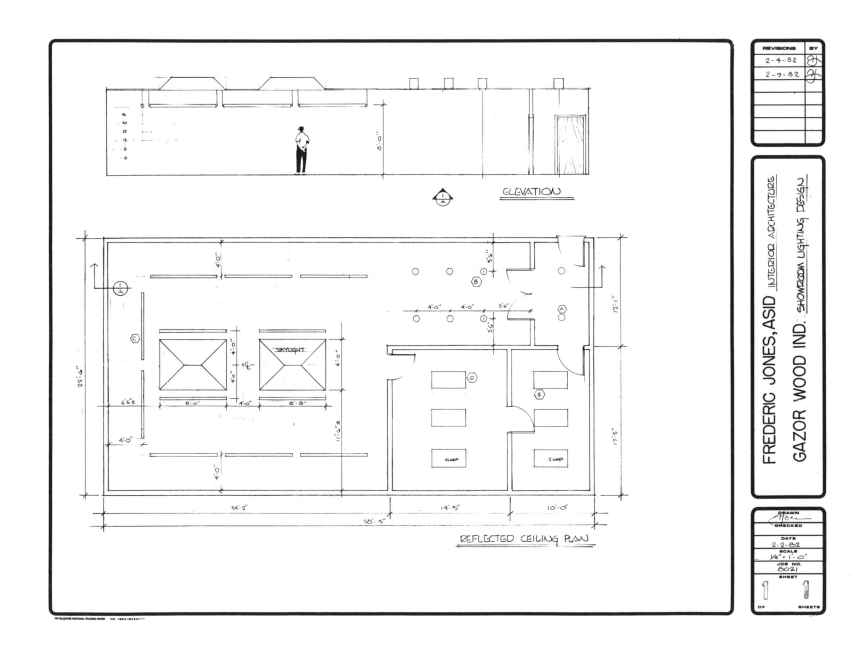

ELEVATION

REFLECTED CEILING PLAN

FREDERIC JONES, ASID INTERIOR ARCHITECTURE
GAZOR WOOD IND. SHOWROOM LIGHTING DESIGN

REVISIONS	BY
2-4-82	
2-9-82	

DRAWN
CHECKED
DATE
2-2-82
SCALE
¼" = 1'-0"
JOB NO.
8021
SHEET
1 OF 1 SHEETS

WORK STATION STANDARD

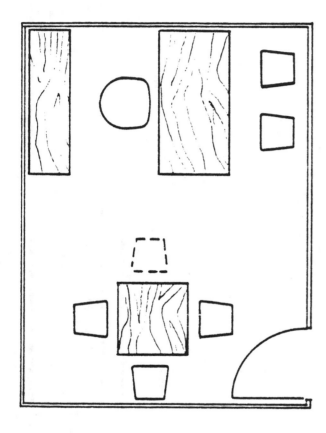

6B

Desk, 36" x 72"
Credenza, 20" x 72"
Visitor Chairs
Conference Table, 36" sq.
Conference Chairs

192

6B

WORK STATION STANDARD

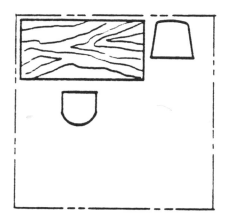

2A

Desk, 30" x 60"

Visitor Chair

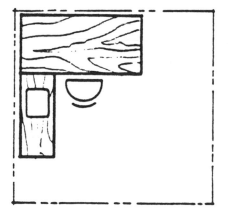

2B

Desk with Return

30" x 60"
with 42" Return

64

2A,B

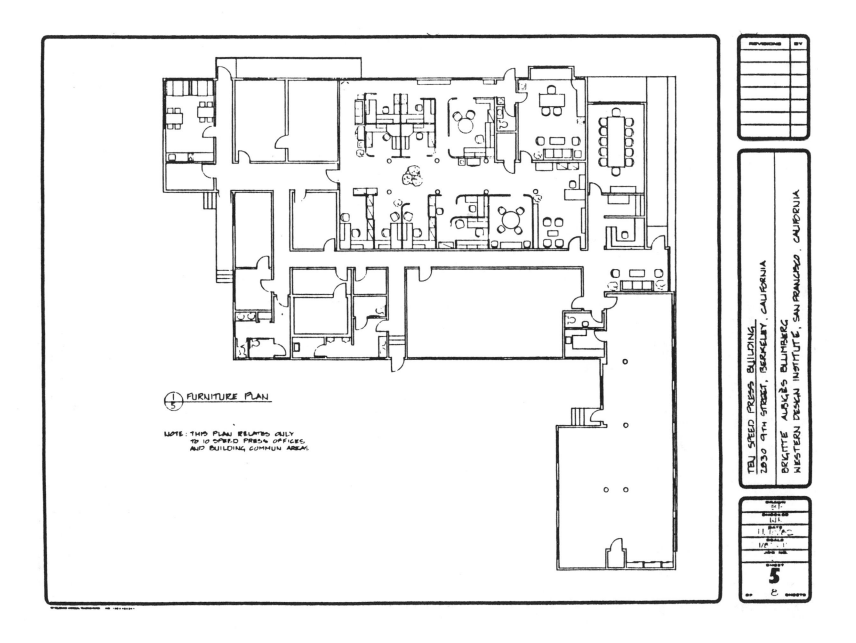

1/5 FURNITURE PLAN

NOTE: THIS PLAN RELATES ONLY
TO 10 SPEED PRESS OFFICES
AND BUILDING COMMUN AREAS

TEN SPEED PRESS BUILDING
2830 9TH STREET, BERKELEY, CALIFORNIA

BRIGITTE AUBGÈS BLUMBERG
WESTERN DESIGN INSTITUTE, SAN FRANCISCO, CALIFORNIA

SHEET
5

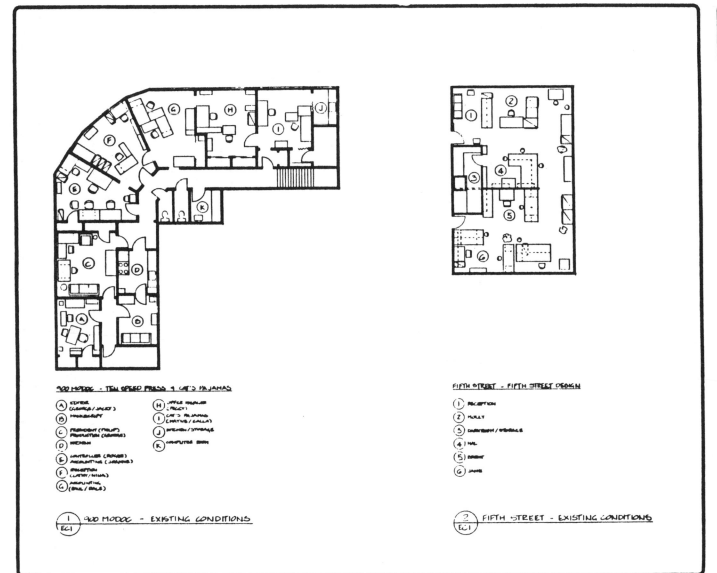

900 MODOC - TEN SPEED PRESS & CAT'S PAJAMAS

(A) EDITOR
(GEORGE / JACKY)

(B) MANUSCRIPT

(C) PRESIDENT (TROUT)
PRODUCTION (JENKINS)

(D) DESIGN

(E) CONTROLLER (ROGER)
ACCOUNTING (JENNING)

(F) RECEPTION
(CATHY / NINA)

(G) ACCOUNTING
(BILL / DALE)

(H) OFFICE MANAGER
(PEGGY)

(I) CAT'S PAJAMAS
(MATILE / CALLA)

(J) KITCHEN / STORAGE

(K) COMPUTER ROOM

FIFTH STREET - FIFTH STREET DESIGN

(1) RECEPTION

(2) MOLLY

(3) DARKROOM / STORAGE

(4) HAL

(5) BRENT

(6) JAMIE

(1/EC1) 900 MODOC - EXISTING CONDITIONS

(2/EC1) FIFTH STREET - EXISTING CONDITIONS

SCALE

2830 NINTH STREET, BERKELEY, CALIFORNIA   JANUARY 1983

WDI GROUP I, WESTERN DESIGN INSTITUTE
SAN FRANCISCO, CALIFORNIA

DRAWN
MAD
CHECKED
WR
DATE
12/29/82
SCALE
1/8" = 1'
JOB NO.

SHEET
EC1

OF 6 SHEETS

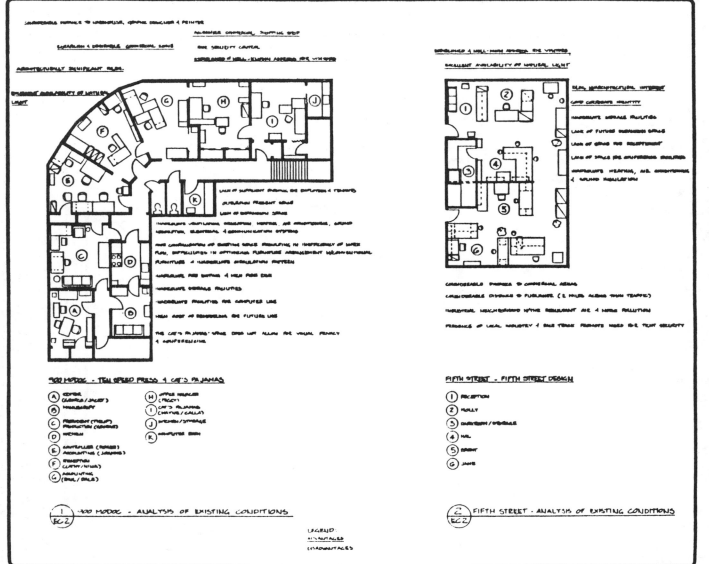

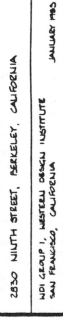

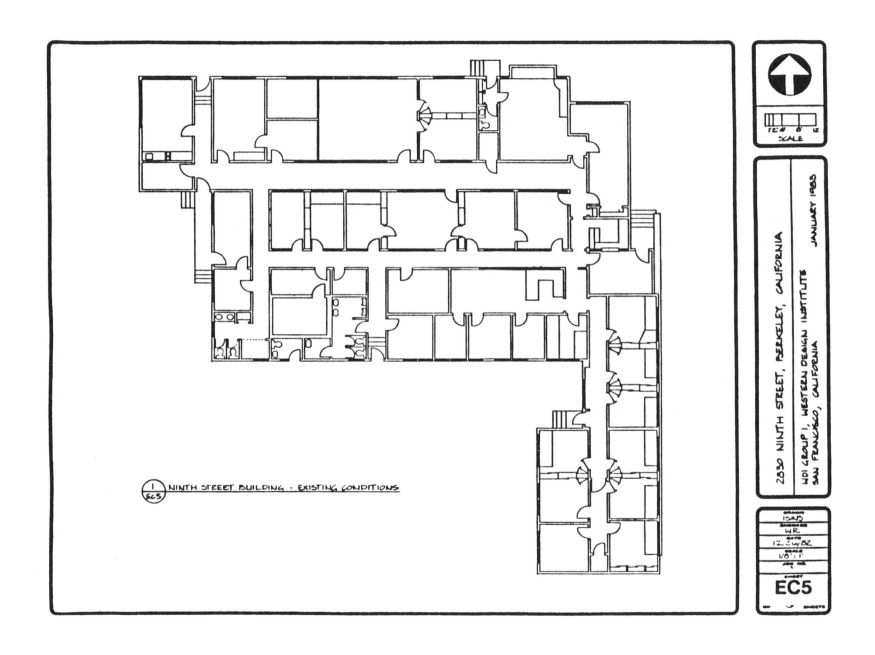

NINTH STREET BUILDING - EXISTING CONDITIONS

2030 NINTH STREET, BERKELEY, CALIFORNIA

WDI GROUP I, WESTERN DESIGN INSTITUTE
SAN FRANCISCO, CALIFORNIA

JANUARY 1983

EC5

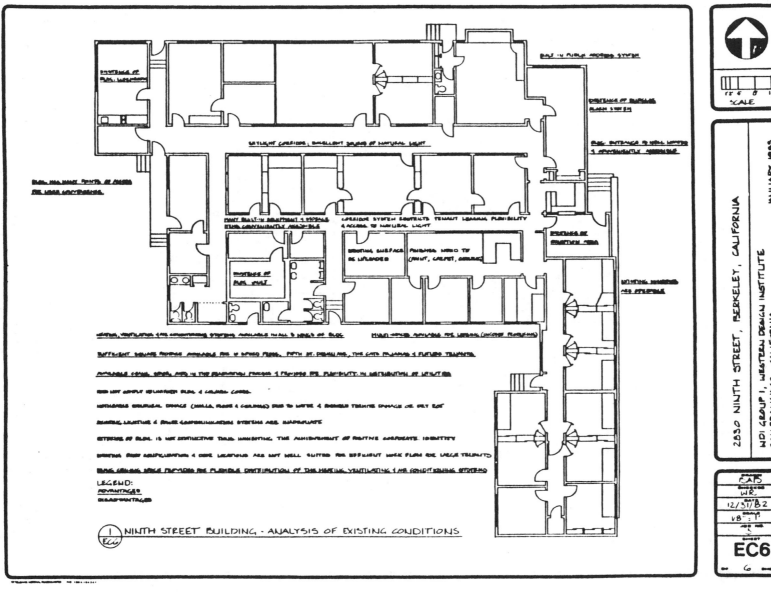

NINTH STREET BUILDING - ANALYSIS OF EXISTING CONDITIONS

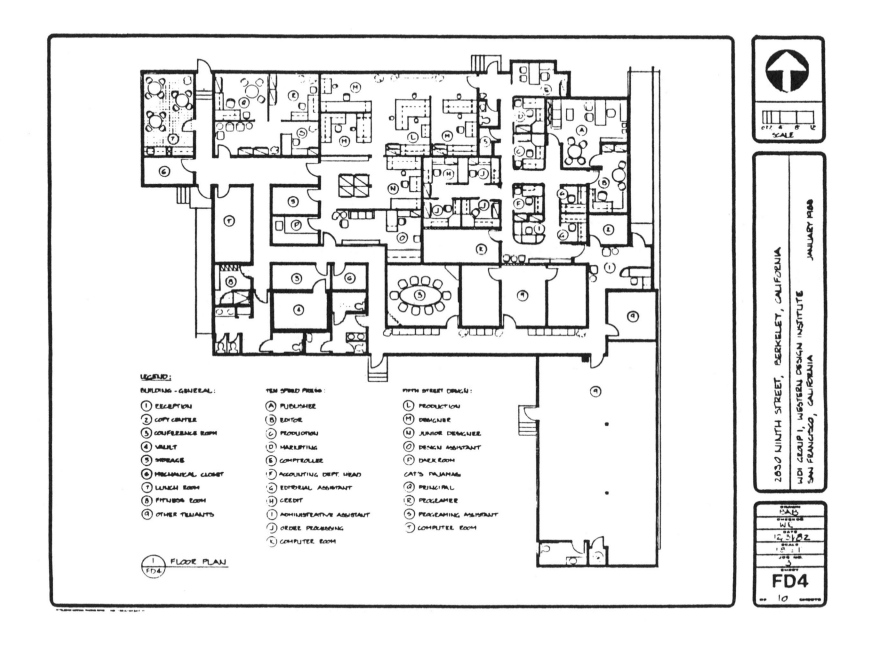

LEGEND:

BUILDING - GENERAL:

1. RECEPTION
2. COPY CENTER
3. CONFERENCE ROOM
4. VAULT
5. STORAGE
6. MECHANICAL CLOSET
7. LUNCH ROOM
8. FITNESS ROOM
9. OTHER TENANTS

TEN SPEED PRESS:

A. PUBLISHER
B. EDITOR
C. PRODUCTION
D. MARKETING
E. COMPTROLLER
F. ACCOUNTING DEPT. HEAD
G. EDITORIAL ASSISTANT
H. CREDIT
I. ADMINISTRATIVE ASSISTANT
J. ORDER PROCESSING
K. COMPUTER ROOM

FIFTH STREET DESIGN:

L. PRODUCTION
M. DESIGNER
N. JUNIOR DESIGNER
O. DESIGN ASSISTANT
P. DARK ROOM

CAT'S PAJAMAS:

Q. PRINCIPAL
R. PROGRAMER
S. PROGRAMING ASSISTANT
T. COMPUTER ROOM

1/FD4 FLOOR PLAN

2030 NINTH STREET, BERKELEY, CALIFORNIA

JANUARY 1988

WDI GROUP I, WESTERN DESIGN INSTITUTE
SAN FRANCISCO, CALIFORNIA

SCALE

DRAWN BAB
CHECKED WL
DATE 12-31-82
SCALE 12:1
JOB NO. 3
SHEET

FD4

OF 10 SHEETS

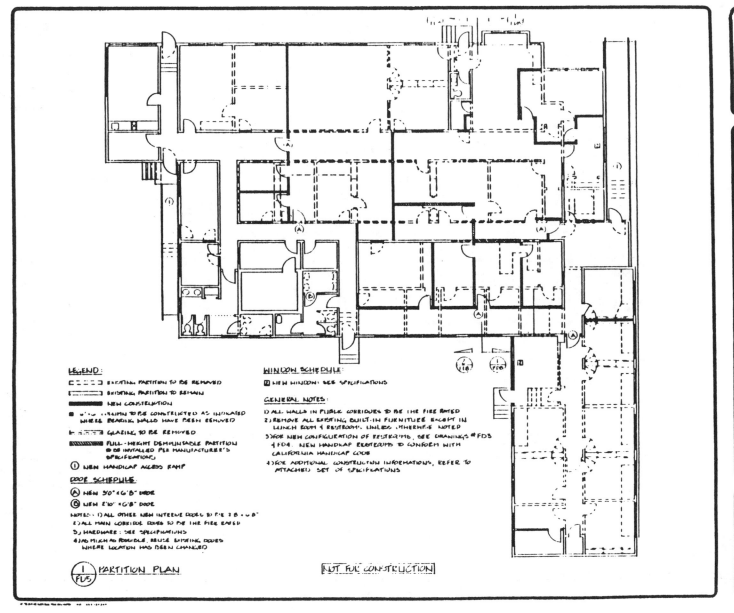

LEGEND:

- ⊏⊐⊏⊐ EXISTING PARTITION TO BE REMOVED
- ▭ EXISTING PARTITION TO REMAIN
- ▬▬ NEW CONSTRUCTION
- ■ WALL PARTITION TO BE CONSTRUCTED AS INDICATED WHERE BEARING WALLS HAVE BEEN REMOVED
- ⊏⊐ GLAZING TO BE REMOVED
- ▨▨ FULL-HEIGHT DEMOUNTABLE PARTITION TO BE INSTALLED PER MANUFACTURER'S SPECIFICATIONS
- ⓘ NEW HANDICAP ACCESS RAMP

DOOR SCHEDULE:

- Ⓐ NEW 3'0" x 6'8" DOOR
- Ⓒ NEW 2'10" x 6'8" DOOR

NOTES: 1) ALL OTHER NEW INTERIOR DOORS TO BE 2'8" x 6'8"
2) ALL MAIN CORRIDOR DOORS TO BE 1HR FIRE RATED
3) HARDWARE: SEE SPECIFICATIONS
4) AS MUCH AS POSSIBLE, REUSE EXISTING DOORS WHERE LOCATION HAS BEEN CHANGED

WINDOW SCHEDULE:

- ▭ NEW WINDOW: SEE SPECIFICATIONS

GENERAL NOTES:

1) ALL WALLS IN PUBLIC CORRIDORS TO BE 1HR FIRE RATED
2) REMOVE ALL EXISTING BUILT-IN FURNITURE EXCEPT IN LUNCH ROOM & RESTROOM, UNLESS OTHERWISE NOTED
3) FOR NEW CONFIGURATION OF RESTROOMS, SEE DRAWINGS # FD3 & FD4. NEW HANDICAP RESTROOMS TO CONFORM WITH CALIFORNIA HANDICAP CODE
4) FOR ADDITIONAL CONSTRUCTION INFORMATIONS, REFER TO ATTACHED SET OF SPECIFICATIONS

① / FD5 — PARTITION PLAN

NOT FOR CONSTRUCTION

2830 NINTH STREET, BERKELEY, CALIFORNIA

WDI GROUP   WESTERN DESIGN INSTITUTE
SAN FRANCISCO, CALIFORNIA

JANUARY 1983

DRAWN	P.A.N.
CHECKED	H.K.
DATE	1/14/83
SCALE	1/8" = 1'
JOB NO	3
SHEET	**FD5**
OF 1 SHEETS	

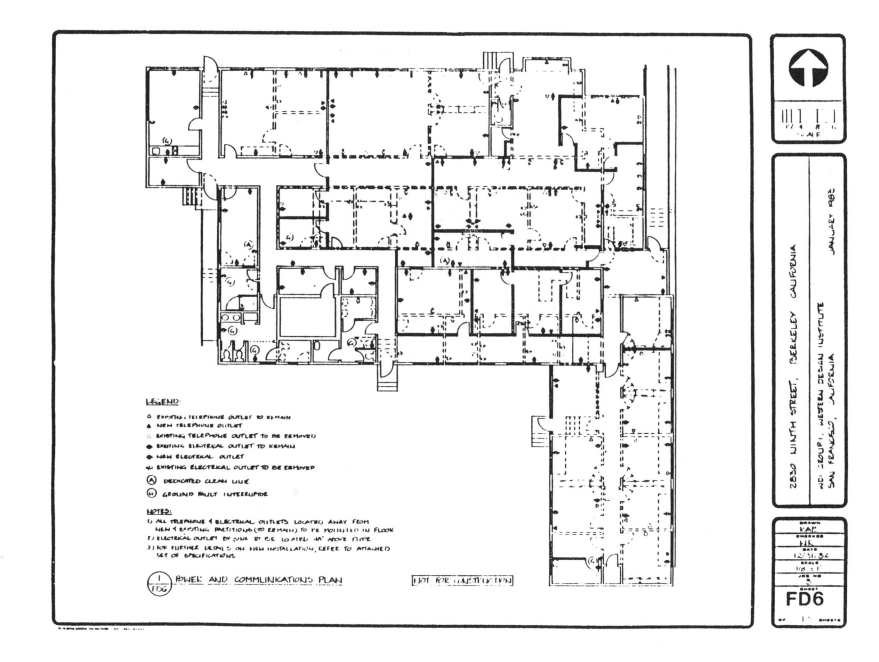

LEGEND:

◦ EXISTING TELEPHONE OUTLET TO REMAIN
▲ NEW TELEPHONE OUTLET
⊙ EXISTING TELEPHONE OUTLET TO BE REMOVED
● EXISTING ELECTRICAL OUTLET TO REMAIN
◉ NEW ELECTRICAL OUTLET
⊘ EXISTING ELECTRICAL OUTLET TO BE REMOVED
Ⓐ DEDICATED CLEAN LINE
Ⓖ GROUND FAULT INTERRUPTOR

NOTES:
1) ALL TELEPHONE & ELECTRICAL OUTLETS LOCATED AWAY FROM
   NEW & EXISTING PARTITIONS (TO REMAIN) TO BE MOUNTED IN FLOOR
2) ELECTRICAL OUTLET BY SINK TO BE LOCATED 48" ABOVE FLOOR
3) FOR FURTHER DETAILS ON NEW INSTALLATION, REFER TO ATTACHED
   SET OF SPECIFICATIONS

1/FD6 POWER AND COMMUNICATIONS PLAN

NOT FOR CONSTRUCTION

2850 NINTH STREET, BERKELEY CALIFORNIA

NO. GROUP 1, WESTERN DESIGN INSTITUTE
SAN FRANCISCO, CALIFORNIA

JANUARY 1982

DRAWN
KAP
CHECKED
HR
DATE
12/31/82
SCALE
1/8" = 1'
JOB NO
5
SHEET
FD6
OF   SHEETS

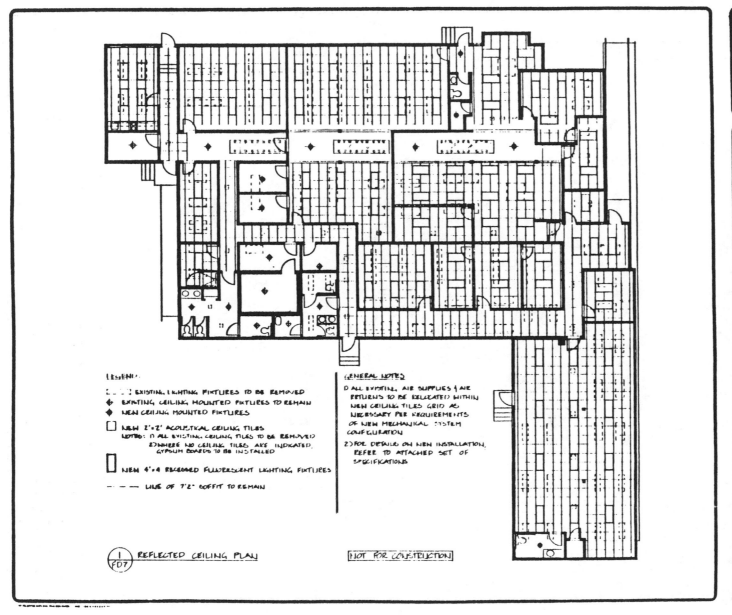

LEGEND:

[ ] EXISTING LIGHTING FIXTURES TO BE REMOVED

◆ EXISTING CEILING MOUNTED FIXTURES TO REMAIN

◆ NEW CEILING MOUNTED FIXTURES

☐ NEW 2'×2' ACOUSTICAL CEILING TILES
NOTE: 1) ALL EXISTING CEILING TILES TO BE REMOVED
2) WHERE NO CEILING TILES ARE INDICATED,
GYPSUM BOARDS TO BE INSTALLED

☐ NEW 4'×4' RECESSED FLUORESCENT LIGHTING FIXTURES

— — — LINE OF 7'2" SOFFIT TO REMAIN

GENERAL NOTES

1) ALL EXISTING AIR SUPPLIES & AIR
RETURNS TO BE RELOCATED WITHIN
NEW CEILING TILES GRID AS
NECESSARY PER REQUIREMENTS
OF NEW MECHANICAL SYSTEM
CONFIGURATION

2) FOR DETAILS ON NEW INSTALLATION,
REFER TO ATTACHED SET OF
SPECIFICATIONS

(1/FD7) REFLECTED CEILING PLAN

[NOT FOR CONSTRUCTION]

SCALE

2830 NINTH STREET, BERKELEY, CALIFORNIA

WDI GROUP 1, WESTERN DESIGN INSTITUTE
SAN FRANCISCO, CALIFORNIA

JANUARY 1983

DRAWN BAS
CHECKED WK
DATE 1/10.83
SCALE 1/8"=1'
JOB NO 3
SHEET FD7
OF 10 SHEETS

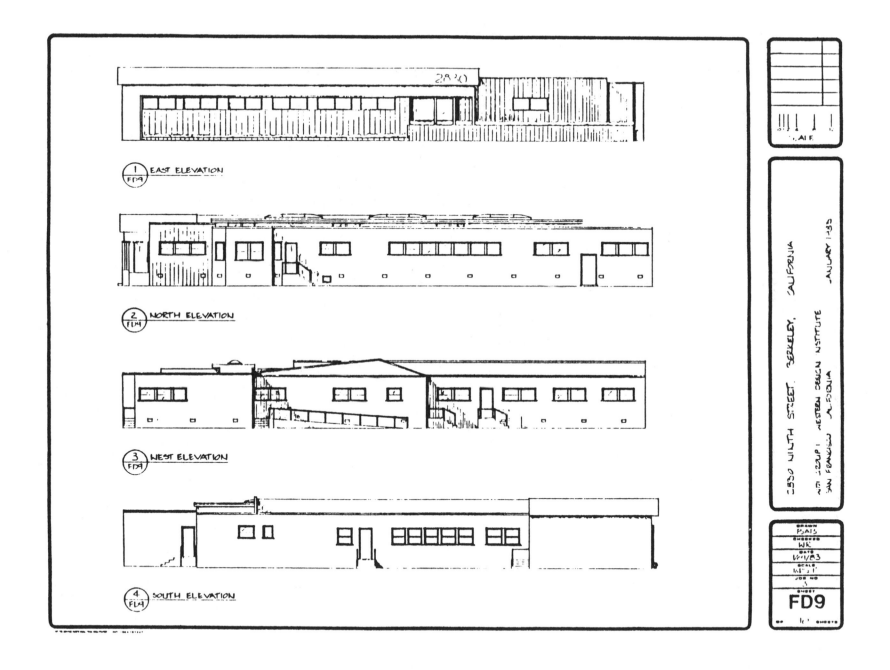

1 EAST ELEVATION
FD9

2 NORTH ELEVATION
FD9

3 WEST ELEVATION
FD9

4 SOUTH ELEVATION
FD9

FD9

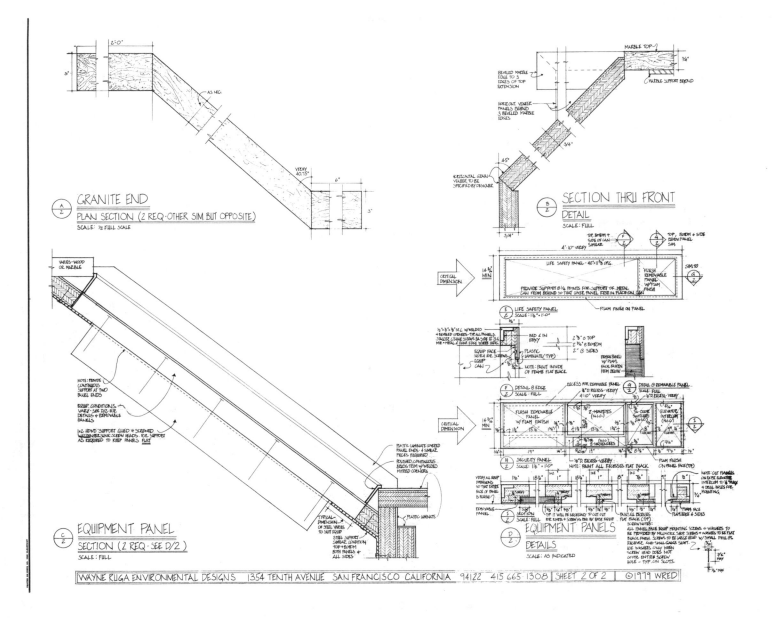

GRANITE END

PLAN SECTION (2 REQ·OTHER SIM. BUT OPPOSITE)
SCALE: ½ FULL SCALE

EQUIPMENT PANEL

SECTION (2 REQ·SEE D/2)
SCALE: FULL

SECTION THRU FRONT

DETAIL
SCALE: FULL

LIFE SAFETY PANEL
SCALE: 1½"=1'-0"

DETAIL @ EDGE
SCALE: FULL

DETAIL @ REMOVABLE PANEL
SCALE: FULL

SECURITY PANEL
SCALE: 1½"=1'-0"

SECTION
SCALE: FULL

EQUIPMENT PANELS

DETAILS
SCALE: AS INDICATED

WAYNE RUGA ENVIRONMENTAL DESIGNS   1354 TENTH AVENUE SAN FRANCISCO CALIFORNIA 94122 415 665 1308 | SHEET 2 OF 2 | ©1979 WRED

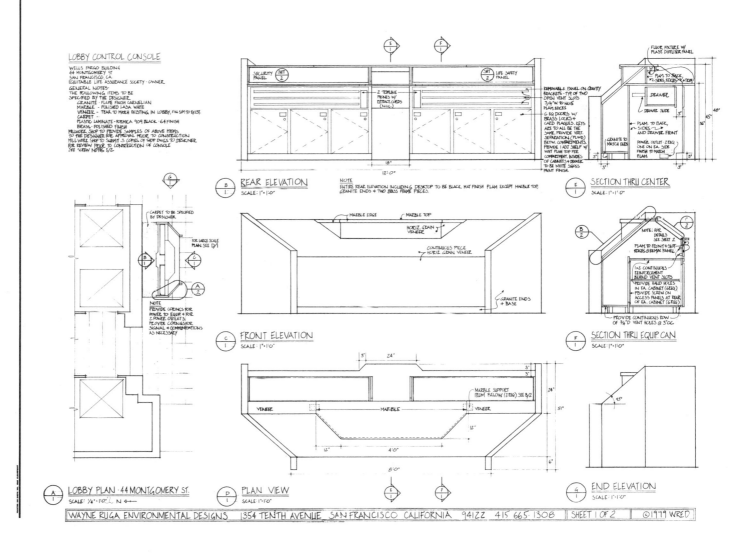

LOBBY CONTROL CONSOLE

WELLS FARGO BUILDING
44 MONTGOMERY ST
SAN FRANCISCO CA.
EQUITABLE LIFE ASSURANCE SOCIETY · OWNER

GENERAL NOTES:
THE FOLLOWING ITEMS TO BE
SPECIFIED BY THE DESIGNER.
  GRANITE - FLAME FINISH CARNELIAN
  MARBLE - POLISHED LASA WHITE
  VENEER - TEAK TO MATCH EXISTING IN LOBBY, FIN. SIM TO EXIST.
  CARPET -
  PLASTIC LAMINATE - FORMICA 909 BLACK · 64 FINISH
  BRASS · POLISHED FINISH
MILLWORK SHOP TO PROVIDE SAMPLES OF ABOVE ITEMS
TO THE DESIGNER FOR APPROVAL PRIOR TO CONSTRUCTION.
MILL WORK SHOP TO SUBMIT 3 COPIES OF SHOP DWGS TO DESIGNER
FOR REVIEW PRIOR TO CONSTRUCTION OF CONSOLE
SEE SCREEN NOTES 1/2

REAR ELEVATION
SCALE: 1" = 1'-0"

NOTE
ENTIRE REAR ELEVATION INCLUDING DESKTOP TO BE BLACK MAT FINISH PLAM EXCEPT MARBLE TOP,
GRANITE ENDS + TWO BRASS FRAME PIECES.

SECTION THRU CENTER
SCALE: 1" = 1'-0"

FRONT ELEVATION
SCALE: 1" = 1'-0"

SECTION THRU EQUIP. CAN
SCALE: 1" = 1'-0"

LOBBY PLAN · 44 MONTGOMERY ST.
SCALE: 1/4" = 1'-0"   N

PLAN VIEW
SCALE: 1" = 1'-0"

END ELEVATION
SCALE: 1" = 1'-0"

WAYNE RUGA ENVIRONMENTAL DESIGNS   1354 TENTH AVENUE   SAN FRANCISCO CALIFORNIA   94122   415 665 1308   ‖ SHEET 1 OF 2 ‖   ©1979 WRED

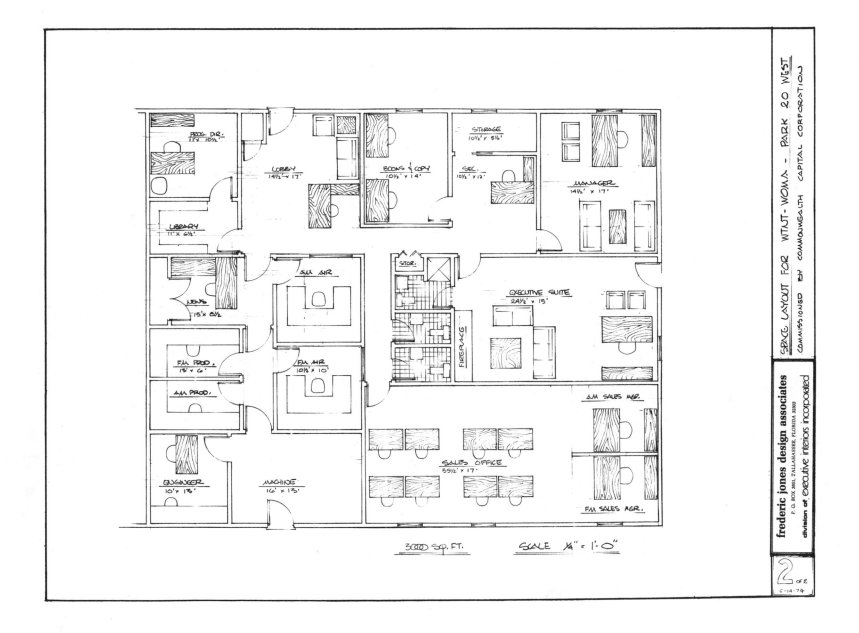

PROG. DIR.
11' x 10½'

LOBBY
14½' x 17'

BOOKS & COPY
10½' x 14'

STORAGE
10½' x 5½'

SEC.
10½' x 12'

MANAGER
14½' x 17'

LIBRARY
11' x 6½'

AM AIR

STOR.

EXECUTIVE SUITE
24½' x 15'

FIREPLACE

NEWS
15' x 8½'

FM PROD.
13' x 6'

FM AIR
10½' x 10'

AM PROD.

AM SALES MGR.

ENGINEER
10' x 13'

MACHINE
16' x 13'

SALES OFFICE
35½' x 17'

FM SALES MGR.

3000 SQ. FT.   SCALE ¼" = 1'-0"

SPACE LAYOUT FOR WTUT-WOMA – PARK 20 WEST
COMMISSIONED BY COMMONWEALTH CAPITAL CORPORATION

frederic jones design associates
P. O. BOX 3851, TALLAHASSEE, FLORIDA 32303
division of executive interiors incorporated

2 OF 2
5-14-74

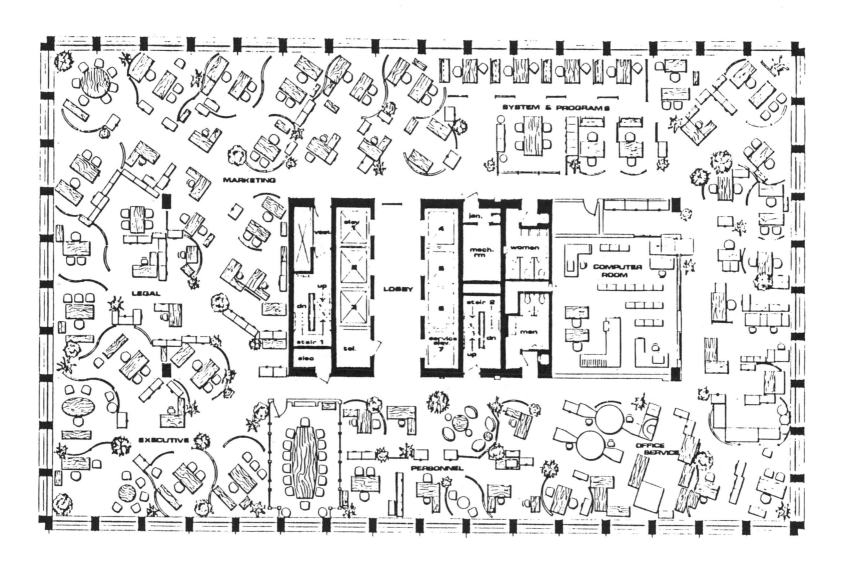

21ˢᵀ FLOOR

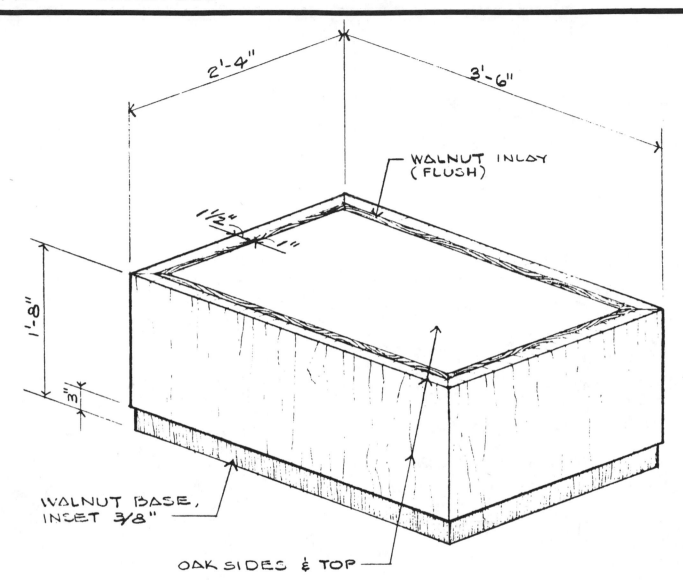

2'-4"

3'-6"

WALNUT INLAY
(FLUSH)

1 1/2"

1"

1'-8"

3"

WALNUT BASE,
INSET 3/8"

OAK SIDES & TOP

NOTE:
DETAILS & FINISH
SHALL MATCH COFFEE
TABLE IN SAME
LOCATION.

END TABLE

RECEPTION AREA, 31ST. FLOOR

ISOMETRIC DRAWING
SCALE: 1"=1'-0"   RMK

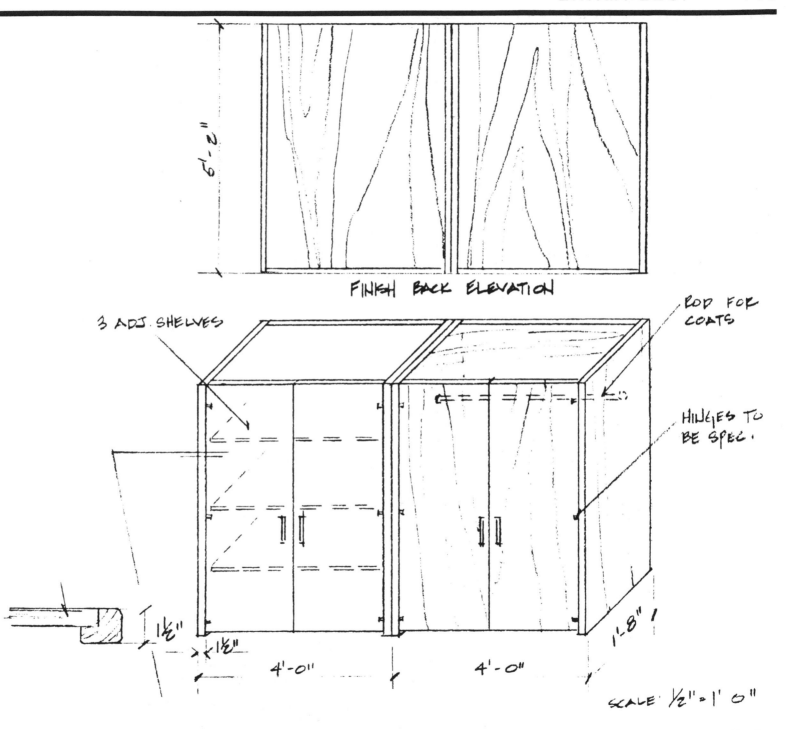

FINISH BACK ELEVATION

6'-2"

3 ADJ. SHELVES

ROD FOR COATS

HINGES TO BE SPEC.

1½"

1½"

1½"

4'-0"

4'-0"

1'-8"

SCALE: ½" = 1' 0"

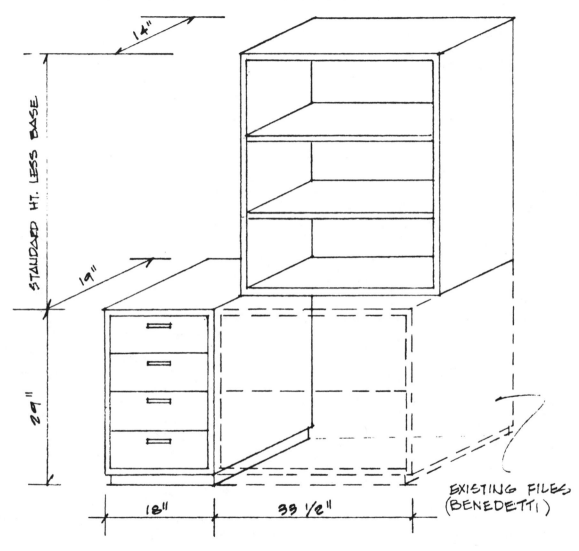

STANDARD HT. LESS BASE

14"

19"

29"

18"

33 1/2"

EXISTING FILES
(BENEDETTI)

ISOMETRIC DRAWING
SCALE : 1/16 = 1'-0"

NEW BOX DRAWER CABINET
AND BOOK CASE
WALNUT · OIL FINISH
DRAWERS · FULL EXTENSION

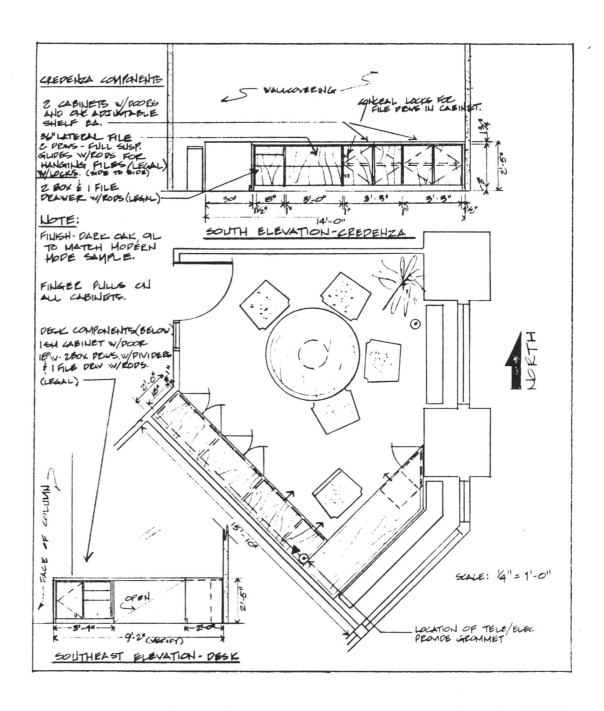

CREDENZA COMPONENTS

2 CABINETS W/DOORS AND ONE ADJUSTABLE SHELF EA.

36" LATERAL FILE 2 DRWS - FULL SUSP. GLIDES W/RODS FOR HANGING FILES (LEGAL) W/LOCKS. (SIDE TO SIDE)

2 BOX & 1 FILE DRAWER W/RODS (LEGAL)

NOTE:

FINISH - DARK OAK, OIL TO MATCH MODERN MODE SAMPLE.

FINGER PULLS ON ALL CABINETS.

DESK COMPONENTS (BELOW) 16" CABINET W/DOOR 18"W - 2 BOX DRWS W/DIVIDERS & 1 FILE DRW W/RODS. (LEGAL)

WALLCOVERING

CONCEAL LOCKS FOR FILE DRWS IN CABINET.

SOUTH ELEVATION - CREDENZA

14'-0"

NORTH

SCALE: 1/4" = 1'-0"

FACE OF COLUMN

OPEN

SOUTHEAST ELEVATION - DESK

9'-2" (VERIFY)

LOCATION OF TELE/ELEC PROVIDE GROMMET

EXISTING CREDENZAS (TO BE MODIFIED):

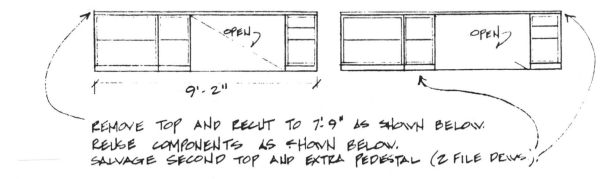

REMOVE TOP AND RECUT TO 7'-9" AS SHOWN BELOW.
REUSE COMPONENTS AS SHOWN BELOW.
SALVAGE SECOND TOP AND EXTRA PEDESTAL (2 FILE DWS.)

NEW CONFIGURATION:

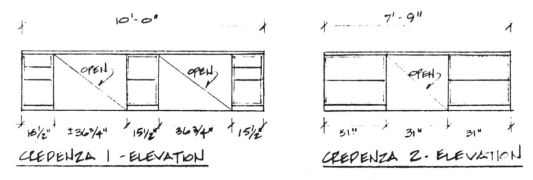

CREDENZA 1 - ELEVATION   CREDENZA 2 - ELEVATION

CR-1 - NEW TOP - 10'-0" L. × 24" D. - PLASTIC LAMINATE TO MATCH EXIST'G.
        REUSE EXIST'G WALNUT PEDESTALS (15½" W.) AS SHOWN.
        ATTACH NEW TOP - LEAVE KNEESPACE AS SHOWN.

CR-2 - RECUT EXIST'G TOP (9'-2") TO 7'-9" × 18" D.
        ATTACH TO EXIST'G WALNUT LATERAL FILES AS SHOWN.

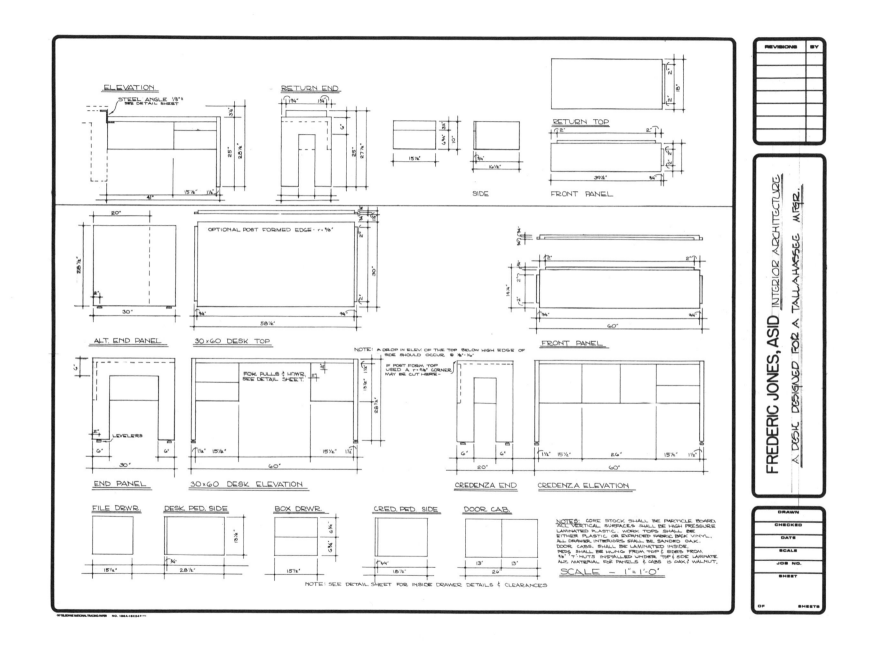

ELEVATION

STEEL ANGLE 1/8"±
SEE DETAIL SHEET

RETURN END

RETURN TOP

SIDE   FRONT PANEL

ALT. END PANEL   30×60 DESK TOP

OPTIONAL POST FORMED EDGE · r· 5/8"

FRONT PANEL

NOTE: A DROP IN ELEV. OF THE TOP BELOW HIGH EDGE OF
SIDE SHOULD OCCUR @ 1/8"-1/4"

IF POST FORM TOP
USED A r· 5/8" CORNER
MAY BE CUT HERE—

FOR PULLS & HDWR,
SEE DETAIL SHEET.

LEVELERS

END PANEL   30×60 DESK ELEVATION

CREDENZA END   CREDENZA ELEVATION

FILE DRWR.   DESK PED. SIDE   BOX DRWR.   CRED. PED. SIDE   DOOR CAB.

NOTES: CORE STOCK SHALL BE PARTICLE BOARD.
ALL VERTICAL SURFACES SHALL BE HIGH PRESSURE
LAMINATED PLASTIC. WORK TOPS SHALL BE
EITHER PLASTIC OR EXPANDED FABRIC BACK VINYL.
ALL DRAWER INTERIORS SHALL BE SANDED OAK.
DOOR CABS. SHALL BE LAMINATED INSIDE.
PEDS. SHALL BE HUNG FROM TOP & SIDES FROM
5/8" "T"-NUTS INSTALLED UNDER TOP & SIDE LAMINATE.
ALT. MATERIAL FOR PANELS & CABS IS OAK & WALNUT.

SCALE – 1"=1'-0"

NOTE: SEE DETAIL SHEET FOR INSIDE DRAWER DETAILS & CLEARANCES

FREDERIC JONES, ASID INTERIOR ARCHITECTURE

A DESK DESIGNED FOR A TALLAHASSEE MTGR.

REVISIONS | BY

DRAWN
CHECKED
DATE
SCALE
JOB NO.
SHEET

OF   SHEETS

RM NO	ROOM DESIGNATION	FLOOR	BASE	WALL / WAINSCOT													CLG / SOFFIT			REMARKS
				NORTH			EAST			SOUTH			WEST							
				MATL	FIN	HT	MATL	FIN	HT	MATL	FIN	HT	MATL	FIN	HT	MATL	FIN	HT	
101	EXAMINATION	E	S	6	X	④	6	X	①	6	X	①	6	X	④				DIA WALL ②
102	EXAMINATION	E	S	6	X	D.O.	6	X	D.O.	6	X	D.O.	6	X	①				DIA WALL ②
103	EXAMINATION	E	S	6	X	D.O.	6	X	D.O.	6	X	D.O.	6	X	D.O.				
104	EXAMINATION	E	S	6	X	D.O.	6	X	③	6	X	D.O.	6	X	D.O.				
105	MENS TOILET	G	F	M	Y	D.O.	M	Z	⑥	M	Y	D.O.	M	Y	⑤				
106	WOMENS TOILET	G	F	M	Y	D.O.	M	Y	①	M	Y	D.O.	M	Z	⑥				
107	OFFICE	C	S	11	X	①	11	X	D.O.	11	X	D.O.	11	X	①				
108	PHARMACY	D	S	6	X	D.O.	6	X	③	6	X	D.O.	6	X	D.O.				
109	PHARMACY STORAGE	D	S	5	X	①	6	X	④A	6	X	D.O.	6	X	D.O.				
110	OPTOMETRY/ WORK	D	S	6	X	①	6	X	①	6	X	D.O.	6	X	④A				
111	OPTOMETRY/ EXAMINATION	E	S	6	X	①	6	X	D.O.	6	X	D.O.	7	X	D.O.				
112	OPTOMETRY/ OFFICE	B	S	11	Y	D.O.	11	X	④	11	X	D.O.	11	X	①				
113	OPTOMETRY/ WORK RM	B	S	11	X	①	11	X	2x6	11	X	2x6	11	X	—				
114	OPTOMETRY/ FITTING	B	S	11	X	2x6	11	X	2x6	11	X	D.O.	11	X	—				
115	OPTOMETRY/ WAITING	B	S	11	XY	①	11	XY	D.O.	11	XY	D.O.	11	XY	⑤				
116	LOBBY	A	S	11	XY	2x6	11	XY	—	11	XY	⑥	11	XY	①				
117	CONSULTATION	B	S	11	XY	①	11	XY	②	11	XY	①	11	XY	④				
118	EXAMINATION	E	S	6	X	D.O.	6	X	①	6	X	D.O.	6	X	②				
119	EXAMINATION	E	S	6	X	D.O.	6	X	D.O.	6	X	D.O.	6	X	①				
120	CONSULTATION	B	S	11	X	D.O.	11	X	⑤	11	X	①	11	X	D.O.				
121	UNIN. TOILET	G	F	Y	M	②	Y	M	2x6	Y	M	①	Y	M	④				
122	TOILET	G	F	Y	M	D.O.	Y	M	①	Y	M	D.O.	Y	M	2x6				
123	DRAW. STATION	D	S	6	X	①	6	X	D.O.	6	X	D.O.	6	X	①				
124	INTERVIEW	B	S	11	XY	D.O.	11	XY	D.O.	11	XY	—	N	Y	D.O.				
125	LAB/WORK AREA	D	S	6	X	D.O.	11	X	D.O.	6	X	—	6	X	?				
126	NURSE STATION	B	S	11	XY	D.O.	11	XY	—	11	XY	①	N	Y	①				
127	SICK CHILD/ WAITING	A	S	11	XY	—	2	XY	①	11	XY	—	0	XY	④				PAINT THE ELEVATOR DOOR 11
128	INTERVIEW	B	S	11	XY	①	11	XY	D.O.	11	XY	①	N	Y	①				
129	CENTRAL WAIT.	A	S	11	XY	D.O.	11	XY	D.O.	11	XY	D.O.	11	XY	D.O.				
130	ADMITTING	H	S	J	XY	D.O.	11	XY	D.O.	11	XY	D.O.	11	XY	D.O.				
131	STERILIZATION	D	S	6	X	D.O.	5	X	D.O.	6	X	④	6	X	①				DOOR / STAIRS ②
132	SOILED HOLDING	D	S	5	X	②	5	X	D.O.	5	X	①	5	X	①				
133	CONSULTATION	B	S	11	X	②	11	X	②	11	X	D.O.	11	X	D.O.				
134	EXAMINATION	E	S	6	X	①	6	X	①	6	X	D.O.	6	X	②				
135	EXAMINATION	E	S	6	X	D.O.	6	X	D.O.	6	X	D.O.	6	X	①				
136	CONSULTATION	B	S	11	X	D.O.	11	X	③	11	X	D.O.	11	X	D.O.				
137	EXAMINATION	E	S	6	X	D.O.	6	X	①	6	X	④	6	X	D.O.				DIA WALL ②
138	EXAMINATION	E	S	6	X	D.O.	6	X	⑤	6	X	D.O.	6	X	①				DIA WALL ②
139	EXAMINATION	E	S	6	X	D.O.	6	X	③	6	X	D.O.	6	X	②				
140	ADMINISTRATION	C	S	11	X	—	11	X	D.O.	11	X	—	11	X	D.O.				
141	MEDICAL RECORDS	C	S	11	X	—	11	X	D.O.	11	X	④	5	X	⑤				
142	OFFICE	C	S	11	X	②	11	X	—	11	X	①	11	X	—				2x6 STUDS @ STAIR
143	OFFICE	C	S	11	X	①	11	X	①	11	X	④	11	X	⑤				
144	OFFICE	C	S	11	X	①	11	X	④	11	X	D.O.	11	X	②				DOOR ①
145	STAIRS	C	S	11	XY	②	11	XY	①	11	XY	②	11	XY	⑤				
146	CORRIDOR	D	S	11	XY	D.O.	11	XY	—	11	XY	D.O.	11	XY	—				
147	JANITOR	D	S			①			④			D.O.			①				
148	not used																		
150	REFUSE	D	S			EX.			①			①			?				no finish
151	STORAGE	D	S			EX.			EX.						?				
152	STORAGE	D	S			EX.			EX.			EX.			?				
153	ELECT./TEL. EQUIPMENT					①						④			?				
154	MEETING	C	S	11	X	④	11	X	②	11	X	④	11	X	?				PAINTED STRIPE EAST/SOUTH/WEST
155	not used	C	S	8	X		8	X		8	X		8	X					
156	not used																		
157	LOCKERS					④			④			①			④				
158	PLAYROOM					D.O.			②			②							

RM NO	ROOM DESIGNATION	FLOOR	BASE	WALL / WAINSCOT													CLG / SOFFIT			REMARKS
				NORTH			EAST			SOUTH			WEST							
				MATL	FIN	HT	MATL	FIN	HT	MATL	FIN	HT	MATL	FIN	HT	MATL	FIN	HT	
159	RADIOLOGY	D	S	6	X	⑩	5	X	⑨	6	X	⑥	6	X	⑨				
160	VIEWING	D	S	6	X	⑥	6	X	①	6	X	②	6	X	①				
161	DARK ROOM	D	S	6	X	D.O.	6	X	⑦	6	X	D.O.	6	X	①				
162	WAITING	B	S	11	XY	—	11	XY	①	11	XY	①	11	XY	①				
163	OFFICE	C	S	11	X	②	11	X	⑦	11	X	①	11	X	—				
164	NURSES STATION	C	S	11	X	—	11	X	—	11	X	④	11	X	—				
165	OFFICE	C	S	11	X	②	11	X	①	11	X	④	11	X	⑨				
166	OFFICE	C	S	11	X	④	11	X	②	11	X	①	11	X	D.O.				
167	OFFICE	C	S	11	X	①	11	X	②	11	X	⑦	11	X	D.O.				
168	TREATMENT	D	S	6	X	④	6	X	④	6	X	②	6	X	②				
169	not used																		
170	CAST ROOM	D	S	6	X	②	6	X	①	6	X	⑨	6	X	D.O.				
171	TOILET	G	F	Y	M	D.O.	Y	M	D.O.	Y	M	①	Y	M	①				
172	AUDIO	D	S	6	X	②	6	X	①	6	X	⑨	6	X	D.O.				
173	STAIRS	C	S	11	XY	—	11	XY	①	11	XY	②	11	XY	①				
201	BUSINESS OFFICE	C	S	11	X		11	X		11	X		11	X					
202	COMPUTER RM.	C	S	11	X		11	X		11	X		11	X					
203	OFFICE	C	S	11	X		11	X		11	X		11	X					
204	OFFICE	C	S	11	X		11	X		11	X		11	X					
205	CONFERENCE RM.	A	S	Y	P		Y	P		Y	P		Y	P					
206	OFFICE	B	S	11	X		11	X		11	X		11	X					
207	"	B	S	11	X		11	X		11	X		11	X					
208	"	B	S	Y	Q		11	X		11	X		11	X					
209	"	B	S	11	X		11	X		11	X		11	X					
210	"	B	S	11	X		11	X		11	X		11	X					
211	STAIR	C	S	11	XY		11	XY		11	XY		11	XY					
212	OFFICE	B	S	11	X		11	X		11	X		11	X					
213	"	B	S	11	X		11	X		Y	K		11	X					
214	"	C	S	11	X		11	X		11	X		11	X					
215	MARKETING	C	S	11	X		11	X		11	X		11	X					
216	WORK RM	C	S	11	X		11	X		11	X		11	X					
217	OFFICE	C	S	11	X		11	X		11	X		11	X					
218	OFFICE	C	S	3	X		3	X		3	X		3	X					
219	STORAGE	D	S	6	X		6	X		6	X		6	X					
220	WOMEN	G	F	Y	M		Y	M		Z	F		Y	M					
221	MEN	G	F	Z	F		Y	M		Y	M		Y	M					
222	STAIR	C	S	11	XY		11	XY		11	XY		11	XY					
223	JANITOR	D	S	6	X		6	X		6	X		6	X					
224	STAFF LOUNGE	D	S	5	X		5	X		5	X		5	X					
225	ELEVATOR	A	S	B	B		B	B		B	B		B	B					CARPET WALLS
226	COPY RM.	D	S	6	X		6	X		6	X		6	X					
227	OFFICE	C	S	11	X		11	X		11	X		11	X					
228	"	C	S	11	X		11	X		11	X		11	X					
229	WAITING	C	S	2	S		2	S		2	S		2	S					
230	SHOWER	G	F	F	Z		F	Z		F	Z		F	Z					

JONES & FELDMAN DESIGN ASSOCIATES · ROCKRIDGE ALBANY

1500 1st STREET, SAN FRANCISCO, CA. 94105   ROCKRIDGE HEALTH CARE PLAN, INC.

FINISH SCHEDULE

REVISIONS	BY
11/29/82	

DRAWN	G.F.
CHECKED	
DATE	10-5-82
SCALE	N.S.
	108.42

SHEET 5 OF 5 SHEETS

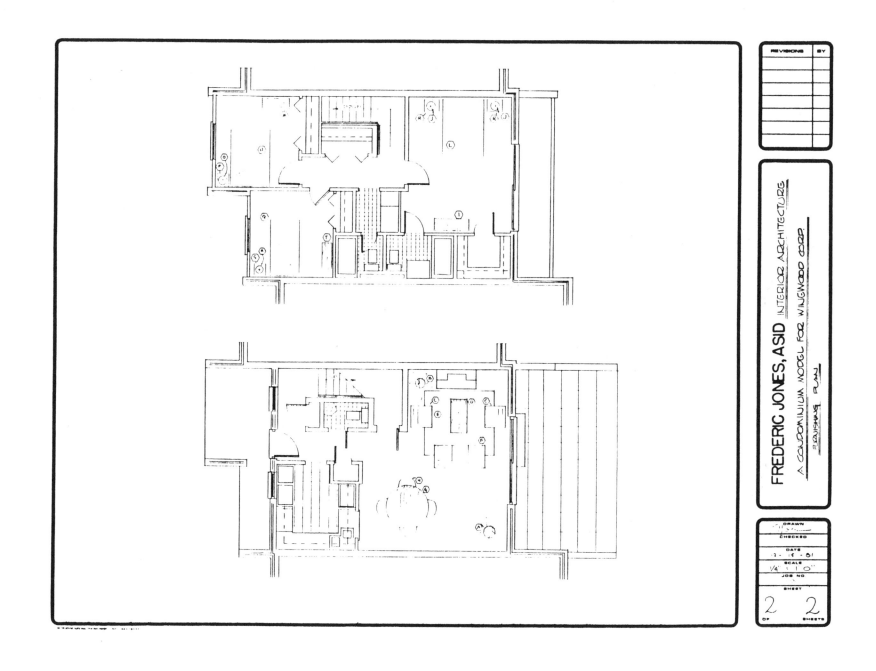

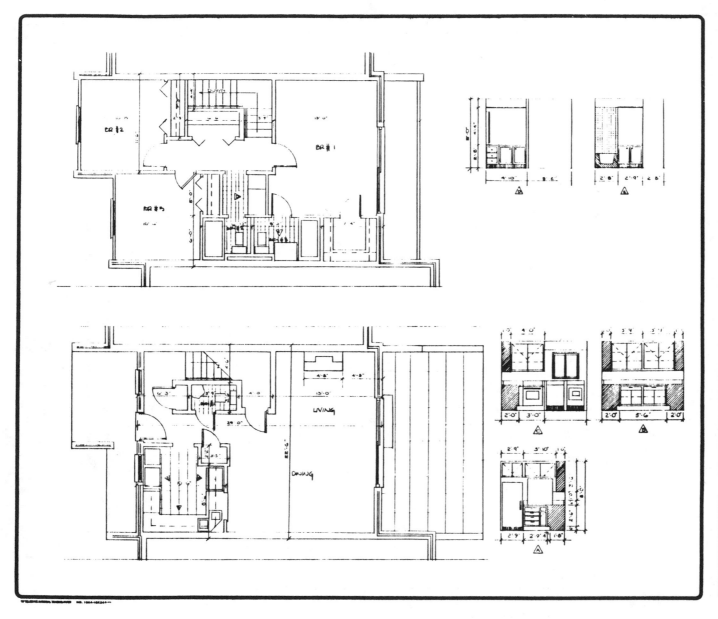

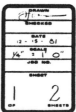

FREDERIC JONES, ASID INTERIOR ARCHITECTURE

A CONDOMINIUM MODEL FOR WINEWOOD CORP.

CONSTRUCTION PLAN & INTERIOR ELEVATIONS

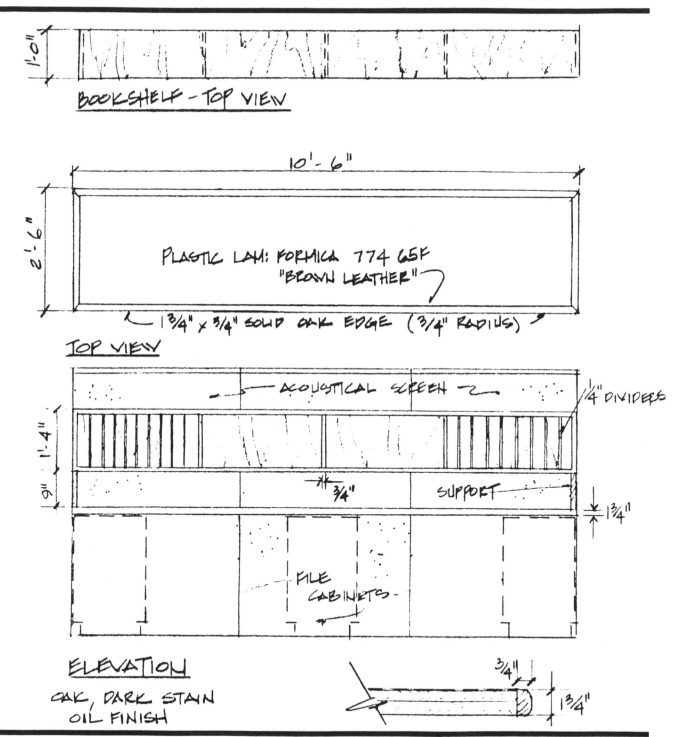

1'-0"

BOOKSHELF - TOP VIEW

10'-6"

2'-6"

PLASTIC LAM: FORMICA 774 G5F
"BROWN LEATHER"

1 3/4" x 3/4" SOLID OAK EDGE (3/4" RADIUS)

TOP VIEW

ACOUSTICAL SCREEN

1/4" DIVIDERS

1'-4"

9"

3/4"   SUPPORT

1 3/4"

FILE
CABINETS

ELEVATION

OAK, DARK STAIN
OIL FINISH

3/4"

1 3/4"

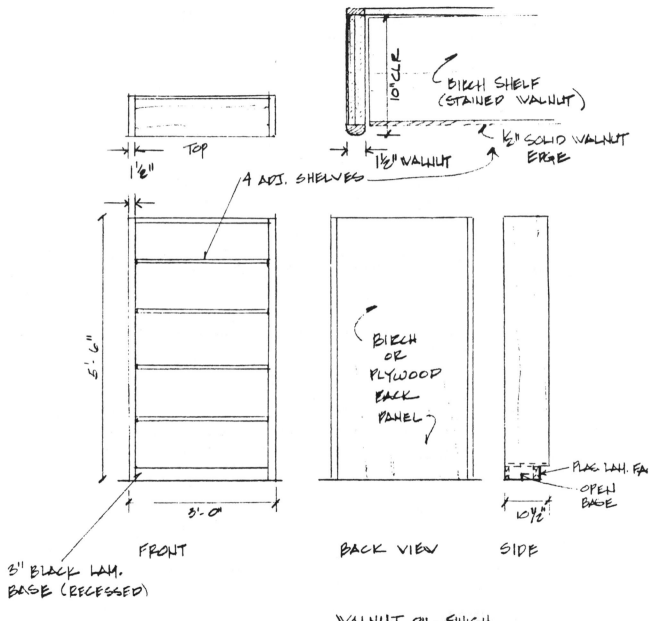

TOP

1½"

10" CLR

BIRCH SHELF
(STAINED WALNUT)

1½" WALNUT

½" SOLID WALNUT
EDGE

4 ADJ. SHELVES

BIRCH
OR
PLYWOOD
BACK
PANEL

5'·6"

3'·0"

PLAS. LAM. FA.

OPEN
BASE

10½"

3" BLACK LAM.
BASE (RECESSED)

FRONT   BACK VIEW   SIDE

WALNUT, OIL FINISH

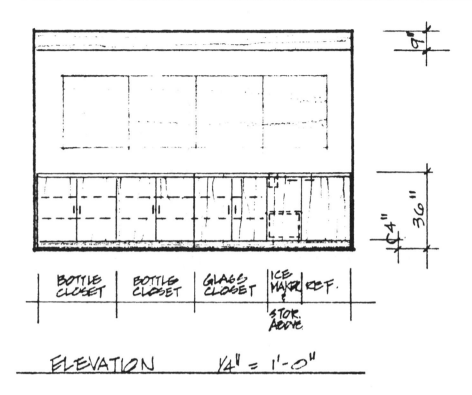

BOTTLE CLOSET	BOTTLE CLOSET	GLASS CLOSET	ICE MAKER & STOR. ABOVE	REF.

ELEVATION $\frac{1}{4}$" = 1'-0"

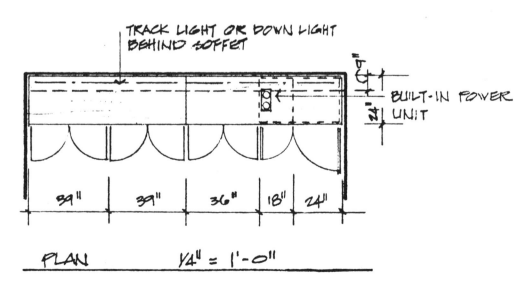

TRACK LIGHT OR DOWN LIGHT BEHIND SOFFET

BUILT-IN POWER UNIT

39"	39"	36"	18"	24"

PLAN $\frac{1}{4}$" = 1'-0"

LIST OF PLATES

Used with permission of:

Pages 23 and 24
Steelcase Corporation

Page 25
L and B Corporation

Page 27
American Radiator and Standard Sanitary Corporation
Copyright 1959

Page 29
King/Reiff and Associates, Architects
Palo Alto, Ca.

Pages 31 and 33
The Pella/Rolscreen Co.

Pages 73, 79, 80, 81, 82, 83, 84, 85, 86, 87, 88, 89
Reproduced from the Manual of Millwork
Published by the Woodwork Institute of California

Pages 98, 99, 100, 101, 102, 103, 104, 105, 106, 107
Western Design Institute
Brigitte Blumberg, Student Project

Pages 108 and 109
Wayne Ruga, Environmental Design
San Francisco, Ca.

Pages 111, 112, 113, 114, 115, 116, 121, 122, 123
Kennedy/Bowen Associates, Inc
San Francisco, Ca.

Unless noted above, all the illustrations in this book are
by the author.

BIBLIOGRAPHY

Ching, Frank. Architectural Graphics. New York: Van Nostrand Reinhold, 1975.

De Chiara, Joseph. Handbook of Architectural Details for Commercial Buildings.
   New York: McGraw-Hill, Inc., 1980.

Diekman, Norman, and Pile, John. Drawing Interior Architecture. New York:
   Whitney Library of Design, (imprint of Watson-Guptil Publications), 1983.

Kicklighter, Clois E., and Baird, Ronald J. Architecture: Residential Drawing
   and Design.   South Holland (Illinois):   The Goodheart-Wilcox Co., 1973.

Olin, Harold B., Schmidt, John L., and Lewis, Walter H. Construction: Principles,
   Materials, and Methods. Chicago: Institute of Financial Education, 1975.

Panero, Jules. Anatomy for Interior Designers. New York: Whitney Publishers.

Panero, Jules, and Zelnik, Martin. Human Dimension and Interior Space. New York:
   Whitney Library of Design (imprint of Watson-Guptill Publications), 1979.

Ramsey, Charles G. and Sleeper, Harold R. Architectural Graphic Standards, 8th
   Edition. New York: John Wiley & Sons, Inc., 1980.

Wakita, Osamu A. and Linde, Richard M. The Professional Practice of Architectural Detailing. New York: John Wiley and Sons, 1977.

Designed by Frederic Jones
Printed offset by Malloy Lithographing Inc.,
Ann Arbor, Michigan on sixty pound
Glatfelter Spring Forge